Music Fundamentals

through pitch structures and rhythmic design

 Ardsley House Publishers, Inc.

Elvo S. D'Amante
Laney Community College

Address editorial correspondence to:
Ardsley House, Publishers
4720 Boston Way
Lanham, MD 20706

ISBN: 1-880157-12-8

Printed in the United States of America

To my wife, Mary

CONTENTS

Preface   xiii
Acknowledgements   xv

CHAPTER 1

The Basics of Pitch and Rhythm   1

Section 1 Pitch Considerations   2

THE STAFF   2
THE CLEF   2
LEDGER LINES   3
THE GREAT STAFF   4
IDENTICAL PITCHES   5

Section 2 The Notation of Rhythm   7

NOTE VALUES AND REST VALUES   7
DOTS AND TIES   7
MANUSCRIPT TIPS   8

Manuscript Practice   10
Drill Studies   12
Assignment for Chapter 1   21

CHAPTER 2

The Tonal Arrangement and Rhythm   23

Section 1 Pitch Considerations   24

THE KEYBOARD   24
HALF STEPS   24
INTERVAL DISTANCES   25
LETTER PLACEMENT   26
ACCIDENTALS   27
ENHARMONIC CONSIDERATIONS   31

Section 2 The Notation of Rhythm   34

TIME SIGNATURES   34
MANUSCRIPT TIPS   37

Manuscript Practice   37
Drill Studies   39
Assignment for Chapter 2   43

CHAPTER 3

Chromatic Scales and Rhythm   45

Section 1 Pitch Considerations   46

THE CHROMATIC SCALE   46

Section 2 The Notation of Rhythm   48

THE METRONOME   48
ABBREVIATED TIME SIGNATURES   49
MANUSCRIPT TIPS   49
A SUGGESTED METHOD OF STUDY   51

Manuscript Practice   52
Drill Studies   55

Assignment for Chapter 3   59
Performance Assignment for Chapter 3   61

CHAPTER 4

Modal Scales and Rhythm   63

Section 1   Pitch Considerations   64

MODAL SCALES   64
MODAL-SCALE SYNTHESIS   66

Section 2   The Notation of Rhythm   68

REVIEW OF BASIC CONCEPTS   68
SIMPLE TIME   69
EQUAL DIVISION   69
THE SPLIT   70
MANUSCRIPT TIPS   71
BEAMS   71

Manuscript Practice   74
Drill Studies   77
Assignment for Chapter 4   85
Performance Assignment for Chapter 4   87

CHAPTER 5

Major Scales and Rhythm   89

Section 1   Pitch Considerations   90

DIATONIC MAJOR SCALES   90
THE MAJOR TETRACHORD   90
KEY SIGNATURES   92
NOTATING MAJOR SCALES   92
THE USE OF ACCIDENTALS   96

Section **2** The Notation of Rhythm   97

OVER THE SPLIT   97
EXCEPTIONS TO EQUAL DIVISION   97
MANUSCRIPT TIPS   99

Manuscript Practice   100
Drill Studies   103
Assignment for Chapter 5   111
Performance Assignment for Chapter 5   113

CHAPTER 6

Minor Scales and Rhythm   115

Section **1** Pitch Considerations   116

DIATONIC MINOR SCALES   116
THE AEOLIAN, HARMONIC, AND MELODIC FORMS   116
THE PARALLEL SYSTEM   118
THE RELATIVE SYSTEM   119
A REVIEW OF MINOR SCALES   123
THE DOMINANT HARMONIC MINOR TETRACHORD   123
A METHOD FOR DETERMINING MINOR KEY SIGNATURES   124

Section **2** The Notation of Rhythm   125

THE USE OF REST VALUES   125
THE WHOLE REST   125
THE HALF REST   126
THE QUARTER REST   127
NOTE-VALUE AND REST-VALUE ERRORS   127
DOTTING RESTS IN SIMPLE TIME   129
MANUSCRIPT TIPS   129

Manuscript Practice   130
Drill Studies   133
Assignment for Chapter 6   141
Performance Assignment for Chapter 6   143
    Dictation Drills and Performance Exercise Answers   146

CHAPTER 7

Major-Scale Interval Identification and Rhythm

147

Section 1 Pitch Considerations 148

MELODIC INTERVALS AND HARMONIC INTERVALS 148
NUMERICAL IDENTIFICATION 148
SIMPLE AND COMPOUND INTERVALS 149
DIATONIC INTERVALS 150

Section 2 The Notation of Rhythm 152

COMPOUND TIME 152
THE UNIT OF MEASURE IN COMPOUND TIME 152
COMPOUND-TIME SIGNATURES 153
DETERMINING THE MODE OF PERFORMANCE 153
GROUPING IN COMPOUND METER 155
THE USE OF REST VALUES IN COMPOUND METER 156
MANUSCRIPT TIPS 157

Manuscript Practice 158
Drill Studies 161
Assignment for Chapter 7 165
Performance Assignment for Chapter 7 167

CHAPTER 8

Chromatic-Interval Identification and Rhythm

169

Section 1 Pitch Considerations 170

CHROMATIC INTERVALS 170
INTERVAL INVERSION 171
INTERVALS OF ENHARMONIC EQUIVALENCY 173

Section 2 The Notation of Rhythm   175

BORROWED DIVISION   175
THE PERFORMANCE OF TRIPLETS AND DUPLETS   175
MANUSCRIPT TIPS   177

Manuscript Practice   179
Drill Studies   181
Assignment for Chapter 8   189
Performance Assignment for Chapter 8   191

CHAPTER 9

Whole-Tone Pentatonic Scales and Rhythm

193

Section 1 Pitch Considerations   194

THE WHOLE-TONE SCALE   194
WRITING WHOLE-TONE SCALES   195
THE PENTATONIC SCALE   197
THE TRITONE   197
WRITING PENTATONIC SCALES   199
INSTANT MODAL TRANSPOSITION   200

Section 2 The Notation of Rhythm   202

ANACRUSIS   202
MANUSCRIPT TIPS   203

Manuscript Practice   204
Drill Studies   207
Assignment for Chapter 9   213
Performance Assignment for Chapter 9   215

CHAPTER **10**

Chords and the Short Form   **217**

Section **1** Pitch Considerations   218

THE ALPHABETICAL CHORD SYSTEM   218
CATEGORY I – THE MAJOR TRIAD   219
CATEGORY I – THE MINOR TRIAD   219
CATEGORY I – THE DIMINISHED TRIAD   219
CATEGORY I – THE AUGMENTED TRIAD   220
CATEGORY I – THE DOMINANT-RELATED TRIADS   220
CATEGORY II – THE INTERVAL OF THE SEVENTH   221
CATEGORY II – THE DOMINANT SEVENTH CHORD   222
CATEGORY II – THE ALTERED AND "SUS FOUR"
    DOMINANTS   223
CATEGORY II – THE MINOR SEVENTH CHORDS   223
CATEGORY II – THE HALF-DIMINISHED SEVENTH CHORD 224
CATEGORY II – THE FULLY DIMINISHED SEVENTH CHORD 224
CATEGORY II – THE MAJOR SEVENTH CHORD   225
CATEGORY II – THE MINOR/MAJOR SEVENTH CHORD   226
CHORDAL DERIVATION   226
CHORDAL EPILOGUE   228

Section **2** The Short Form   228

BINARY AND TERNARY FORMS   229
THE *DA CAPO* FORM   229
THE *DAL SEGNO* FORM   230
FIRST AND SECOND ENDINGS   231
MANUSCRIPT TIPS   231

Manuscript Practice   232
Drill Studies   235
Assignment for Chapter 10   242
Performance Assignment for Chapter 10   244

Glossary   247

Performance Terms and Expression Marks   257

Sample Solutions of Selected Drill Studies   261

Index   267

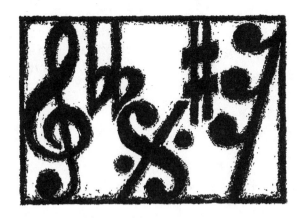

PREFACE

Music Fundamentals through Pitch Structures and Rhythmic Design is intended to serve music majors as well as those students in other disciplines who wish to acquire a working knowledge of musicianship and basic music theory. Additionally, practicing musicians will find its clear approach practical and useful in strengthening and enhancing musical performance.

The book provides a solid and meaningful background to the study of basic musical concepts through two broad and parallel notions: *pitch structures* and *rhythmic design*. The presentation involves the systematic use of four currently used clefs, identical pitches, keyboard illustrations, scales, intervals, triads, seventh chords, note and rest values, as well as the rhythmic concepts of simple and compound meters. In addition, basic areas of musicianship are presented to include experiences in *keyboard performance*, *sight-reading*, and *ear training* with melodic and rhythmic dictation. Features include:

- 128 **musical examples**, which illustrate important concepts
- 15 **tables**, which visually clarify primary relationships
- **manuscript tips**
- **drill studies** for self-testing and monitoring purposes
- **chapter assignments** (on *perforated* sheets), which can be collected as homework
- **performance assignments**
- a **glossary** of musical concepts
- **performance terms** and **expression marks**
- **sample solutions** to selected drill exercises.

A correction booklet with a *midterm* and *final examination* is available to instructors who adopt the text.

The language of music is expressed in a multitude of symbols that attempt to convey pitch, duration, and a desired manner of performance. *Music Fundamentals* presents an opportunity for musical discovery and the achievement of excellence.

ACKNOWLEDGMENTS

Many people have contributed to this project, but I especially wish to thank three music associates for their proofreading skills: Dix Bruce, a former student of mine, who enjoys a professional career in music and is a successful, published author of several music books; Jim Lynch, one of my finest theory students and, lucky for me, a computer expert—he saved many a day; and last, but not least, Jay Lehmann of Laney Community College, a colleague of mine and an exceptionally fine music instructor, who is endowed with a critical eye and who gave me expert advice. I am grateful to the following reviewers, who read over the entire manuscript and made numerous helpful suggestions: Chris Culver of Jacksonville State University, William Munroe of Ferris State University, Fred Squatrito of California State University, Fullerton, and Gerald Woughter of Oakland Community College. Additionally, I would like to thank all of my students, past and present, and my colleagues in the music department at Laney for their valuable suggestions and editorial assistance. Finally, the music used for this book was written in Finale and Music Prose.

I also wish to acknowledge, with admiration and appreciation, the incalculable influence of Darius Milhaud and Roger Sessions with whom I studied—and without whom none of this would have been possible.

CHAPTER 1

The BASICS of PITCH and RHYTHM

Section

1

Pitch Considerations

THE STAFF

Pitch is defined as the high or low quality of sound that is determined, in essence, by its frequency or number of vibrations per second. In contrast to pitch, **duration**, as it relates to rhythmic design, is defined as the maximum or minimum length of time that a given pitch is capable of being sustained. The modern **staff**, which provides the necessary locale for the placement of almost all symbols dealing with pitch, duration, and performance, consists of five horizontal **lines** and four **spaces**. For identification purposes, lines and spaces are numbered progressively from the bottom up. The lines are numbered one through five and the spaces, one through four.

Example 1

The five lines and four spaces of the staff.

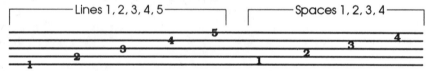

THE CLEF

Pitch names of the staff are taken from the first seven letters of the English alphabet: A, B, C, D, E, F, and G. In addition to numbers, these letter names provide another means to line and space identification. It is, however, the **clef**, a symbol placed on the staff, that actually determines the manner in which these letter names are assigned. The **treble** or **G clef**

generally represents the upper register of musical sounds. In examining this symbol, note carefully how the lower portion of the clef symbol encircles the *second line* on the staff, which represents the pitch G.

Example 2

The treble clef (G clef).

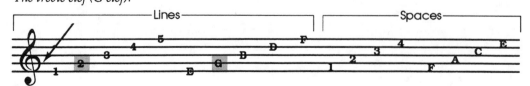

The **bass clef**

which, generally represents the lower register of sounds, is often referred to as the **F clef**. In examining this symbol, note carefully the placement of the *two dots above and below the fourth line*, which represents F.

Example 3
The bass clef (F clef).

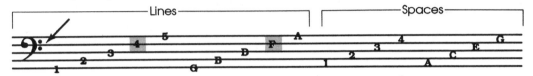

In this text, two additional clefs will be utilized. These clefs are referred to as **movable C clefs**, viz. **alto** and **tenor**. Carefully examine the placement of these clefs, for it is the position of the clef in relationship to the *chosen line* that determines the *alto* (Example 4) or *tenor* clef (Example 5). These clefs are used mainly by musical instruments. The viola uses the alto clef almost exclusively, while virtuoso parts are often written for violoncello using the tenor clef.

Example 4
Alto clef.

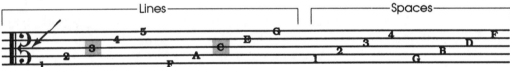

Example 5
Tenor clef.

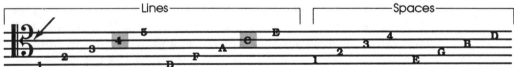

LEDGER LINES

Notes are symbols placed on a staff to indicate the pitches and durations of sounds. Frequently, there is a need to extend the range of a musical staff by writing notes above or below the staff. When this occurs, identification of these pitches is easily achieved through the use of **ledger lines**. These short lines are drawn above or below the staff to represent abbreviated staff lines and thereby extend the range of the lines and spaces. Additionally, when involving pitches that require one or more ledger lines, each added line and space degree must be shown between the desired pitch and the staff. Pitches found on spaces above or below the staff do not require an *additional* line beyond the desired pitch, a common error in music manuscript.

Example 6
The use of ledger lines.

THE GREAT STAFF

Originally the **Great staff** was represented as an eleven-line staff and appeared as follows:

Example 7
The eleven-line staff.

To provide an easier visual pattern, the eleven-line staff was later divided into two groups of five lines each, joined together by a single line on the left; it was braced to the left (a bracket shaped somewhat like an archer's bow) and spaced sufficiently apart to provide for additional pitches and ledger lines, which might be placed between the two staffs. The center line (line six) of the original staff was reduced to a ledger line, only to be used when needed by either clef, and is referred to as the **implied eleventh line**. The spacing arrangement between the two staffs provides a means for extending the lower range of pitches for the upper clef and, in similar fashion, the upper range of pitches for the lower clef. Thus, the first ledger line above the bass staff indicates exactly the same pitch as a note placed on the first ledger line below the treble staff. A note so placed on the implied eleventh line of either staff is called **middle c, c-prime (c')**, or **c-one (c¹)**.

Example 8
The modern Great staff, ledger lines, and middle c.

IDENTICAL PITCHES

The understanding and placement of **identical pitches** (two or more notes representing the same pitch) on a Great staff or a score of mixed clefs can best be learned through the use of the nomenclature and pitch-spectrum guide presented in Table 1, below.

Table 1 illustrates the exact letter name for each pitch of the piano keyboard; it also pinpoints the divisional makeup of **registers** (ranges of sound). The **small** and **prime** (c^1) **registers** are given in their entirety, while all other registers are presented in their abbreviated forms. Register designations are specific and identifiable by their written appearance. The **subcontra, contra,** and **Great** registers are designated with upper-case letters, while the small and prime (numbered registers) utilize lower-case letters. It should be understood that the alto, tenor, and bass clefs, with the aid of ledger lines, also utilize the same corresponding register designations and pitch names.

To understand the concept of identical pitches through the use of clefs, the following information and examples should prove beneficial.

Middle c (c^1), the first line added below the *treble clef*, can be written in *alto clef* as a note placed on the third line, in *tenor clef* as a note placed on the fourth line and, finally, in *bass clef*, as a note placed on the first line added above the staff. All represent exactly the *same pitch* and are referred to in this text as *identical pitches*. See Example 9(a) on page 6.

In Example 9(b), the fourth line in the *bass* clef, lower-case f, can be written in the *treble* clef as the third line added below the staff. In

Table 1 ▪ *Nomenclature and Pitch Spectrum of the Piano*

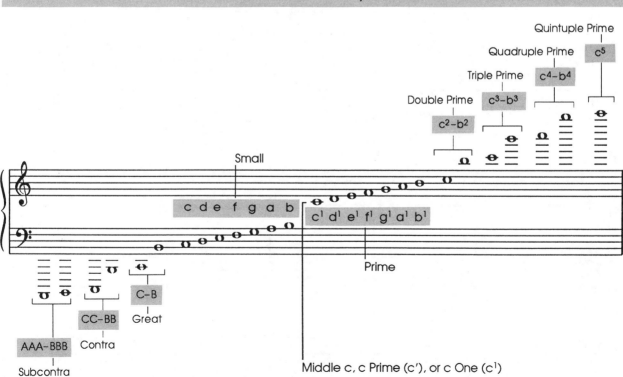

the *alto* clef it can be shown as a note placed on the first line. And in the *tenor* clef lower-case f is placed on the second line. Examine and study the following sets of *identical pitches*, utilizing a score of mixed clefs. Pay careful attention to corresponding registers and to the accurate placement of pitches.

Example 9(a)
Middle c (c¹) as an identical pitch.

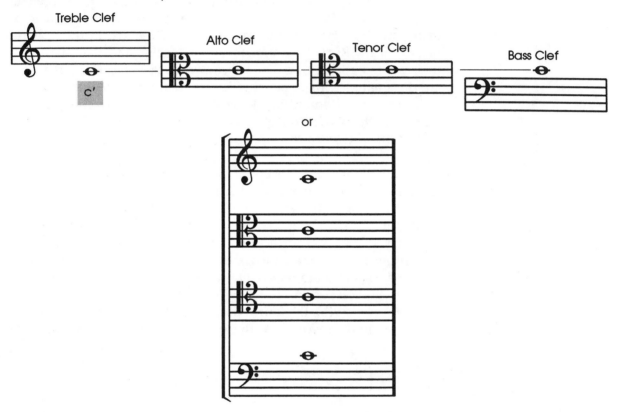

Example 9(b)
Identical pitches.

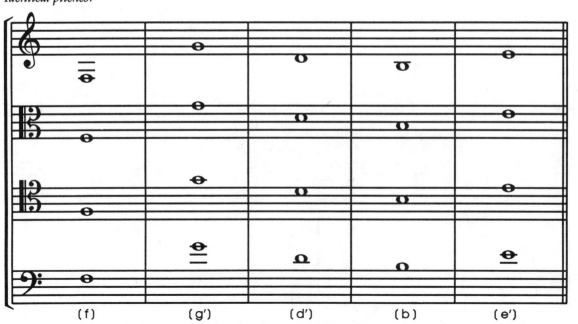

Section

2

The Notation of Rhythm

NOTE VALUES AND REST VALUES

In the study of rhythm, duration of time is represented by a system of symbols that are referred to as *note values* and *rest values*. **Note values** symbolize the duration of time for notes; **rest values** symbolize durations of silence. Table 2 (page 8) presents each duration level used with its symbol, name, and equivalent rest value. The duration of each note-value and rest-value level is half that of the note value and rest value immediately above it.

DOTS AND TIES

Lengthening the duration of note values or rest values can be easily achieved in the notation of rhythm. Two rhythmic devices are used for this purpose. The first one, a dot placed to the right of the **note head** (the circular part of the note symbol) is referred to, simply, as a **dot**. It receives half the value of the note value or rest value that it follows. A second dot would receive half the value of the first dot, and so forth. Although the system of notation allows for the use of more than two dots, rhythmic expressions utilizing additional dots are seldom seen. Because dots are not always desirable in certain rhythmic environments, it is possible to achieve the same result by utilizing the second device, an arc "connecting" the note heads, and referred to as a **tie**. The following example provides a more visual appreciation of how both of these devices work.

Example 10

Dots and ties.

	Table 2 ▪ *Note Values and Rest Values*		
NAME	NOTE-VALUE SYMBOL	REST-VALUE SYMBOL	NAME
Double whole note			Double whole rest
Whole note			Whole rest
Half note			Half rest
Quarter note			Quarter rest
Eighth note			Eighth rest
Sixteenth note			Sixteenth rest
Thirty-second note			Thirty-second rest
Sixty-fourth note			Sixty-fourth rest

MANUSCRIPT TIPS

The following principles are generally observed and adhered to in the notating of rhythm.

1. *Stems and Flags.* In the writing of music manuscript, the length of a **stem** (the vertical line attached to the note head), is approximately one *octave* long. At this point, an **octave** can best be defined as the distance of eight letter names, for example,

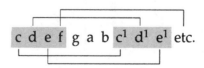

c d e f g a b c^1 d^1 e^1 etc.

(see Table 1). The attachment of the stem to the note head is governed by the placement of the note head on the staff. In **single-line music** (music meant for one voice or one instrument) the *third staff line* plays an important role. Any stemmed note head placed below the third line has its stem attached on the *right side* and pointing *upward*. In contrast, any stemmed note head above the third line has its stem attached to the *left* and pointing *downward*. Stemmed note heads *on* the third line may have their stems pointing up or down and attached accordingly. **Flags**, the curved banner-shaped attachments to the stems, shorten set durations of time and are always placed to the right, whether the stem points downward or upward.

2. *Ties.* The use of ties is governed primarily by most of the rules that affect the placement of stems. Also, ties are drawn from the center of one note head to another—so as not to touch the note heads—and are placed on the side of the note head opposite to the stem.

3. *Dots.* If the note head is on a space, the dot or dots are placed on the same space adjacent to the note head and to its right. If the note head is on a line, the dot or dots are placed adjacent to the note head and immediately to the right on the space above.

4. *Rests.* Double whole rests, whole rests, and half rests are carefully drawn on the staff according to line placement. Be sure to memorize which rest is placed in which position. In manuscript writing, the quarter rest is the only rest that may be creatively drawn; however, every effort should be made to have it look as close to the printed version as possible. Avoid quarter rests that have the appearance of the number "3" or of the upper-case letter "E." Eighth-note, sixteenth-note, thirty-second-note, and sixty-fourth-note rests are drawn on the staff according to space placement. Again, be sure to memorize the line, space, and flag arrangement of each of these rests. Rest symbols are *never* tied. (See Table 2 for quick reference.)

Pay careful attention to Example 11 and to some of the different ways that stems, ties, dots, and rests appear in the writing of music manuscript.

Example 11
Rhythmic symbols of notation.

Manuscript Practice

Use these manuscript pages for note taking and drill.

DRILL STUDY #1

Instructions: In Exercises 1–9, identify the written pitches on the staffs and write their letter names in the individual brackets provided below each note. Be sure that each pitch name is in the proper register. An extra line of brackets has been provided for a repeat of the exercise. *Bracket line 1 should be completed first and then covered when doing bracket line 2.* Refer to the chapter as often as is necessary.

1.

2. ( ) ( ) ( ) ( ) ( ) ( ) ( ) ( ) ( )
DO
BRACKET LINE 1 → 1. ( ) ( ) ( ) ( ) ( ) ( ) ( ) ( ) ( )
FIRST.
THEN COVER AND
DO BRACKET LINE 2.

2.

2. ( ) ( ) ( ) ( ) ( ) ( ) ( ) ( )
1. ( ) ( ) ( ) ( ) ( ) ( ) ( ) ( )

3.

2. ( ) ( ) ( ) ( ) ( ) ( ) ( ) ( )
1. ( ) ( ) ( ) ( ) ( ) ( ) ( ) ( )

4.

2. ( ) ( ) ( ) ( ) ( ) ( ) ( ) ( )
1. ( ) ( ) ( ) ( ) ( ) ( ) ( ) ( )

5.

2. ( ) ( ) ( ) ( ) ( ) ( ) ( ) ( )
1. ( ) ( ) ( ) ( ) ( ) ( ) ( ) ( )

6.

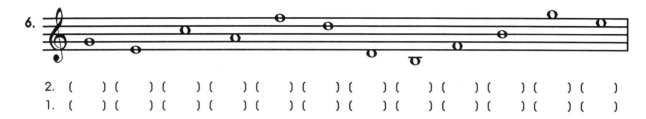

```
2.  (    ) (    ) (    ) (    ) (    ) (    ) (    ) (    ) (    ) (    ) (    )
1.  (    ) (    ) (    ) (    ) (    ) (    ) (    ) (    ) (    ) (    ) (    )
```

7.

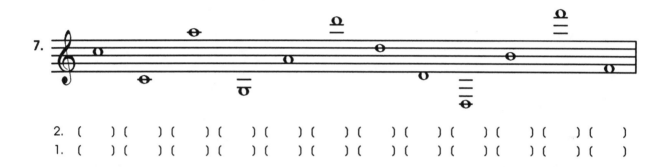

```
2.  (    ) (    ) (    ) (    ) (    ) (    ) (    ) (    ) (    ) (    ) (    )
1.  (    ) (    ) (    ) (    ) (    ) (    ) (    ) (    ) (    ) (    ) (    )
```

8.

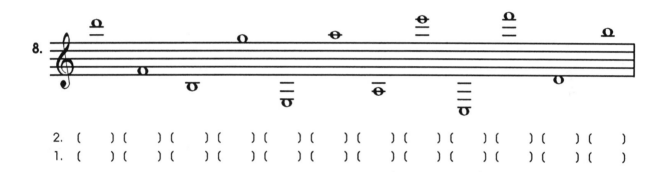

```
2.  (    ) (    ) (    ) (    ) (    ) (    ) (    ) (    ) (    ) (    ) (    )
1.  (    ) (    ) (    ) (    ) (    ) (    ) (    ) (    ) (    ) (    ) (    )
```

9.

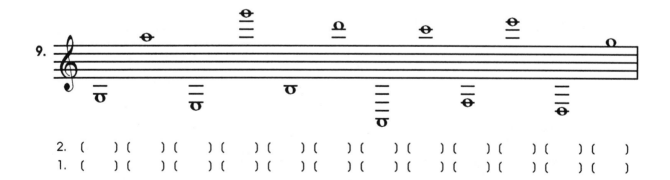

```
2.  (    ) (    ) (    ) (    ) (    ) (    ) (    ) (    ) (    ) (    ) (    )
1.  (    ) (    ) (    ) (    ) (    ) (    ) (    ) (    ) (    ) (    ) (    )
```

When you have checked and studied your responses thoroughly, proceed to the next drill study.

DRILL STUDY #2

Instructions: In Exercises 1–8, use the instructions for Drill Study #1; two additional lines of brackets are provided for extra practice. Each line of brackets should be completed and covered before the line above it is completed.

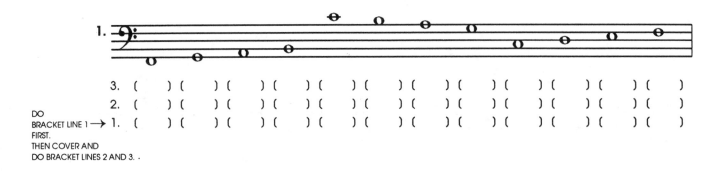

1.

3. ( ) ( ) ( ) ( ) ( ) ( ) ( ) ( ) ( ) ( ) ( ) ( )
2. ( ) ( ) ( ) ( ) ( ) ( ) ( ) ( ) ( ) ( ) ( ) ( )

DO
BRACKET LINE 1 → 1. ( ) ( ) ( ) ( ) ( ) ( ) ( ) ( ) ( ) ( ) ( ) ( )
FIRST.
THEN COVER AND
DO BRACKET LINES 2 AND 3.

2.

3. ( ) ( ) ( ) ( ) ( ) ( ) ( ) ( ) ( ) ( ) ( ) ( )
2. ( ) ( ) ( ) ( ) ( ) ( ) ( ) ( ) ( ) ( ) ( ) ( )
1. ( ) ( ) ( ) ( ) ( ) ( ) ( ) ( ) ( ) ( ) ( ) ( )

3.

3. ( ) ( ) ( ) ( ) ( ) ( ) ( ) ( ) ( ) ( ) ( ) ( )
2. ( ) ( ) ( ) ( ) ( ) ( ) ( ) ( ) ( ) ( ) ( ) ( )
1. ( ) ( ) ( ) ( ) ( ) ( ) ( ) ( ) ( ) ( ) ( ) ( )

4.

3. ( ) ( ) ( ) ( ) ( ) ( ) ( ) ( ) ( ) ( ) ( ) ( )
2. ( ) ( ) ( ) ( ) ( ) ( ) ( ) ( ) ( ) ( ) ( ) ( )
1. ( ) ( ) ( ) ( ) ( ) ( ) ( ) ( ) ( ) ( ) ( ) ( )

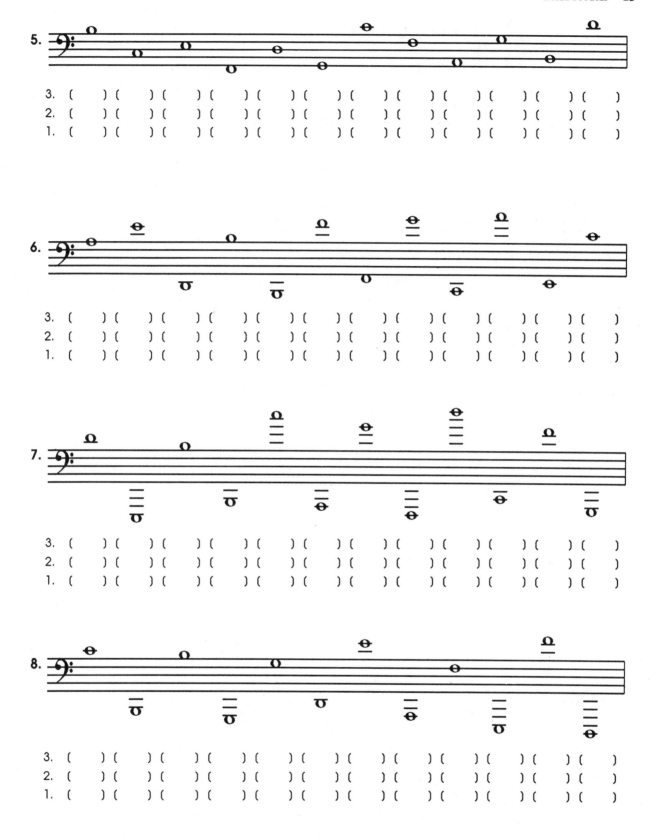

When you have checked and studied your responses thoroughly, proceed to the next drill study.

DRILL STUDY #3

Instructions: In Exercises 1–6, use the instructions for Drill Study #1; three additional lines of brackets have been provided for extra practice. Again, note that each line of brackets should be completed and covered in the same manner as was suggested in previous Drill Studies.

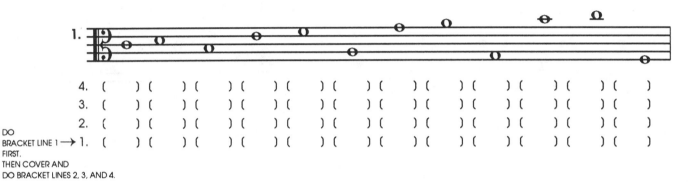

4. ( ) ( ) ( ) ( ) ( ) ( ) ( ) ( ) ( ) ( ) ( )
3. ( ) ( ) ( ) ( ) ( ) ( ) ( ) ( ) ( ) ( ) ( )
2. ( ) ( ) ( ) ( ) ( ) ( ) ( ) ( ) ( ) ( ) ( )

DO
BRACKET LINE 1 → 1. ( ) ( ) ( ) ( ) ( ) ( ) ( ) ( ) ( ) ( ) ( )
FIRST.
THEN COVER AND
DO BRACKET LINES 2, 3, AND 4.

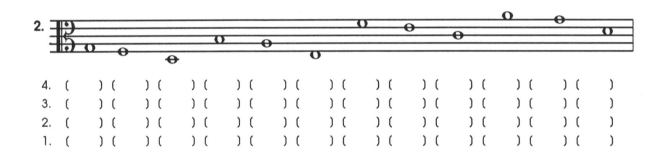

4. ( ) ( ) ( ) ( ) ( ) ( ) ( ) ( ) ( ) ( ) ( )
3. ( ) ( ) ( ) ( ) ( ) ( ) ( ) ( ) ( ) ( ) ( )
2. ( ) ( ) ( ) ( ) ( ) ( ) ( ) ( ) ( ) ( ) ( )
1. ( ) ( ) ( ) ( ) ( ) ( ) ( ) ( ) ( ) ( ) ( )

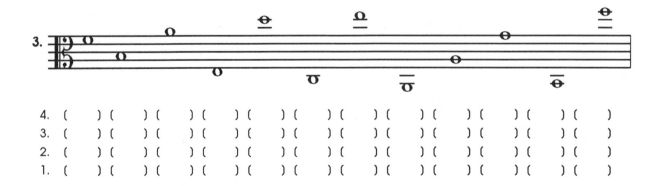

4. ( ) ( ) ( ) ( ) ( ) ( ) ( ) ( ) ( ) ( ) ( )
3. ( ) ( ) ( ) ( ) ( ) ( ) ( ) ( ) ( ) ( ) ( )
2. ( ) ( ) ( ) ( ) ( ) ( ) ( ) ( ) ( ) ( ) ( )
1. ( ) ( ) ( ) ( ) ( ) ( ) ( ) ( ) ( ) ( ) ( )

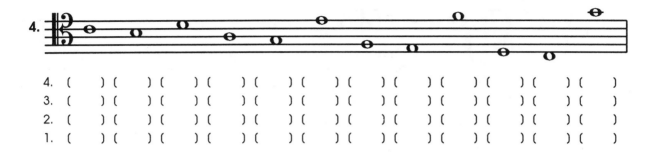

4. ( ) ( ) ( ) ( ) ( ) ( ) ( ) ( ) ( ) ( ) ( ) ( )
3. ( ) ( ) ( ) ( ) ( ) ( ) ( ) ( ) ( ) ( ) ( ) ( )
2. ( ) ( ) ( ) ( ) ( ) ( ) ( ) ( ) ( ) ( ) ( ) ( )
1. ( ) ( ) ( ) ( ) ( ) ( ) ( ) ( ) ( ) ( ) ( ) ( )

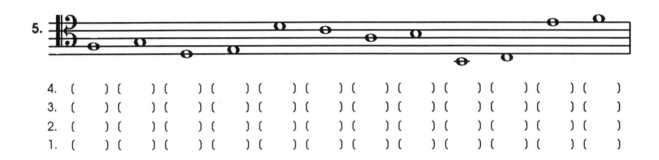

4. ( ) ( ) ( ) ( ) ( ) ( ) ( ) ( ) ( ) ( ) ( ) ( )
3. ( ) ( ) ( ) ( ) ( ) ( ) ( ) ( ) ( ) ( ) ( ) ( )
2. ( ) ( ) ( ) ( ) ( ) ( ) ( ) ( ) ( ) ( ) ( ) ( )
1. ( ) ( ) ( ) ( ) ( ) ( ) ( ) ( ) ( ) ( ) ( ) ( )

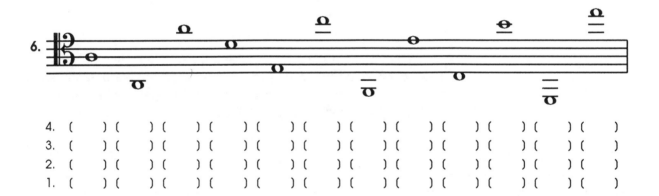

4. ( ) ( ) ( ) ( ) ( ) ( ) ( ) ( ) ( ) ( ) ( ) ( )
3. ( ) ( ) ( ) ( ) ( ) ( ) ( ) ( ) ( ) ( ) ( ) ( )
2. ( ) ( ) ( ) ( ) ( ) ( ) ( ) ( ) ( ) ( ) ( ) ( )
1. ( ) ( ) ( ) ( ) ( ) ( ) ( ) ( ) ( ) ( ) ( ) ( )

When you have checked and studied your responses thoroughly, proceed to the next drill study.

DRILL STUDY #4

1. *Instructions:* In Parts (a)–(d), reproduce each clef several times on the staffs provided. Draw each clef as closely as possible in appearance to the printed clef.

2. *Instructions:* In Parts (a)–(h), identify each note symbol given in the corresponding space provided; also, in the blank staff below, reproduce each note symbol as closely as possible in appearance to the printed symbol.

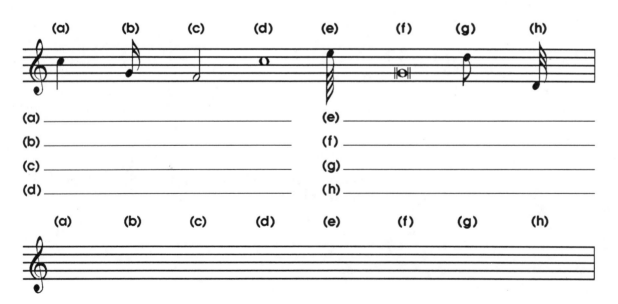

3. *Instructions:* In Parts (a)–(h), identify each rest symbol given in the corresponding space provided; also, in the blank staff below, reproduce each rest symbol as closely as possible in appearance to the printed symbol.

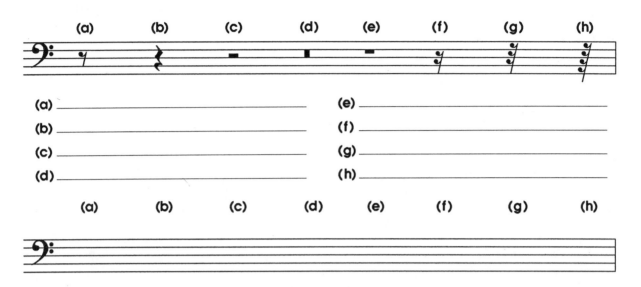

| (a) | (b) | (c) | (d) | (e) | (f) | (g) | (h) |

(a) _____ (e) _____

(b) _____ (f) _____

(c) _____ (g) _____

(d) _____ (h) _____

4. *Instructions:* Parts (a)–(t) are based upon the relative-duration factors of note values and rest values. Fill in the blank spaces in each statement. It might be wise to review Table 2 on page 8.

(a) Quarter notes are half the duration of _____ notes.

(b) _____ rests are half the duration of quarter rests.

(c) Thirty-second rests are half the duration of _____ rests.

(d) _____ notes are half the duration of sixteenth notes.

(e) Sixty-fourth rests are half the duration of _____ rests.

(f) _____ notes are twice the duration of whole notes.

(g) Half rests are twice the duration of _____ rests.

(h) _____ notes are twice the duration of half notes.

(i) Double whole rests are twice the duration of _____ rests.

(j) _____ notes are twice the duration of quarter notes.

(k) Sixteenth rests are twice the duration of _____ rests.

(l) _____ notes are half the duration of whole notes.

(m) Quarter rests are twice the duration of _____ rests.

(n) _____ notes are half the duration of eighth notes.

(o) Whole rests are half the duration of _____ rests.

(p) _____ rests are half the duration of sixteenth rests.

(q) Eighth notes are twice the duration of _____ notes.

(r) _____ notes are twice the duration of eighth notes.

(s) Sixty-fourth notes are half the duration of _____ notes.

(t) _____ rests are twice the duration of sixteenth rests.

ASSIGNMENT FOR CHAPTER 1

NAME _____ SCORE _____ GRADE _____

DATE DUE _____ SECTION _____ INSTRUCTOR _____

1. *Instructions:* In Parts (a)–(e), within the brackets provided below each exercise, identify the name and register of each pitch. Be sure to read the indicated clef correctly and to check your work thoroughly.

(a)

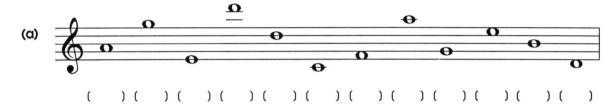

(   ) (   ) (   ) (   ) (   ) (   ) (   ) (   ) (   ) (   ) (   ) (   )

(b)

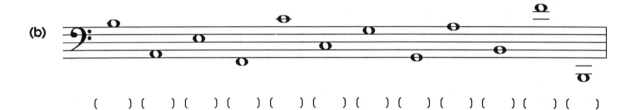

(   ) (   ) (   ) (   ) (   ) (   ) (   ) (   ) (   ) (   ) (   ) (   )

(c)

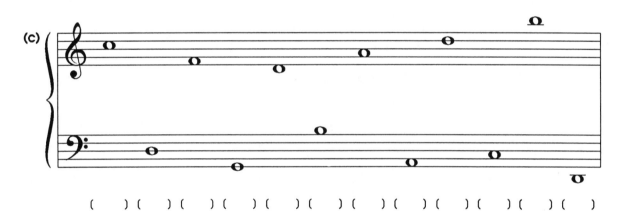

(   ) (   ) (   ) (   ) (   ) (   ) (   ) (   ) (   ) (   ) (   ) (   )

(d)

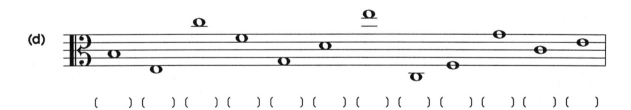

(   ) (   ) (   ) (   ) (   ) (   ) (   ) (   ) (   ) (   ) (   ) (   )

(e)

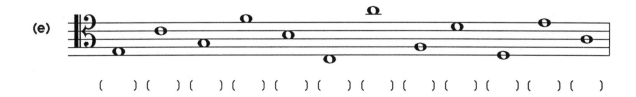

(   ) (   ) (   ) (   ) (   ) (   ) (   ) (   ) (   ) (   ) (   ) (   )

2. *Instructions:* In Parts (a)–(h), place the corresponding note or rest value next to each note or rest value in the staff space provided.

3. *Instructions:* For Parts (a)–(h): On the lower staff, place the symbol that represents half of the note value or rest value on the upper staff.

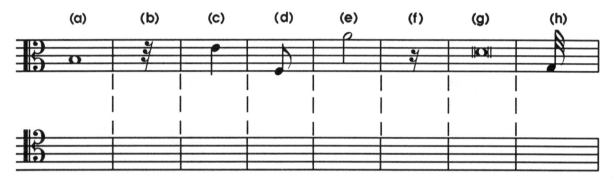

4. *Instructions:* As in the shaded example given on the left, supply the identical pitch for each separate clef on the staffs provided. Immediately below the four staffs, place the exact letter name in the brackets provided. This is an exercise in the concept of identical pitches.

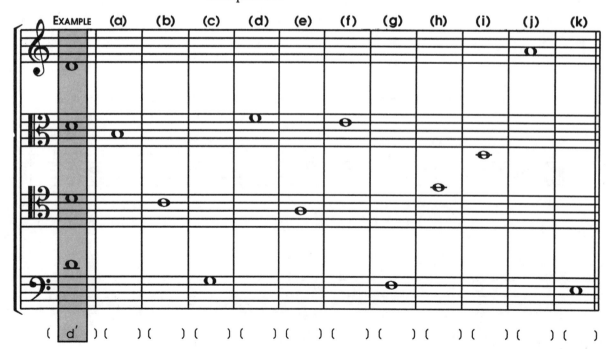

CHAPTER

2

The
TONAL
ARRANGEMENT
and
RHYTHM

Section

1

Pitch Considerations

THE KEYBOARD

Understanding pitch and the ramifications of spatial relationships in music can best be approached by acquiring a knowledge of the tonal arrangement of the piano keyboard. Our modern piano and its keyboard afford not only an aural appraisal of pitches, but also define visual distances of pitch. An **interval**, therefore, is defined in terms of *spatial* distance—namely, the distance of sound between two pitches.

Example 12
Whole steps and half steps on the keyboard.

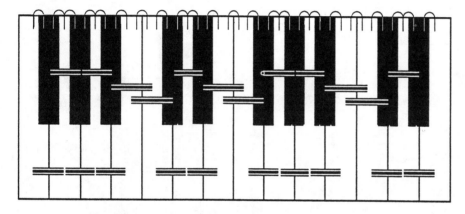

≡ Horizontal lines indicate whole steps.
∩ Curved lines indicate half steps.

HALF STEPS

The smallest intervals of sound encountered in most of the music of our Western civilization and visually prominent on the keyboard are **half steps**. They are found between some of the white keys, but most often, between white keys and their adjacent black keys. In the next example, a series of *half steps* has been assigned numbers to coincide with what is referred to as an *octave*. These piano keys are numbered from one through thirteen. The distance between each piano key and its assigned number represents the interval of one half step. At this point, an **octave** can best be defined as an interval containing twelve half steps. Other *octaves* are bracketed above and below the keyboard in Example 13 for further illustration. Also, it should be understood that an octave contains twelve half steps, but has thirteen individual keyboard steps. The thirteenth key is merely a reiteration of the original starting pitch one octave higher or lower, depending upon whether the scale is ascending or descending.

Example 13
Octaves.

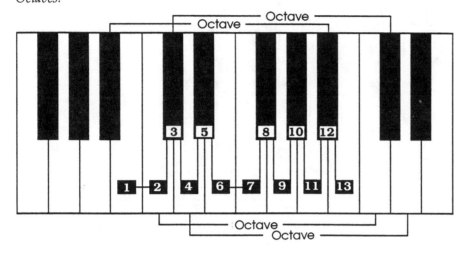

INTERVAL DISTANCES

By combining **whole steps** (intervals of two half steps) and half steps, it is possible to create interval distances of larger or smaller dimensions, as illustrated in Example 14.

Example 14
Interval dimensions.

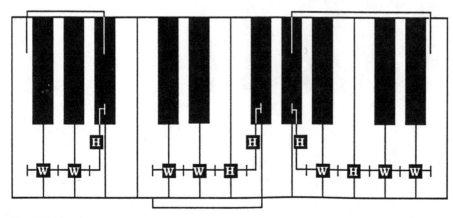

W = Whole step
H = Half step

LETTER PLACEMENT

The alphabetical letter names or letter placement used to identify the lines and spaces of the staff coincide with the white keys of the piano keyboard.

Example 15
White keys of the piano.

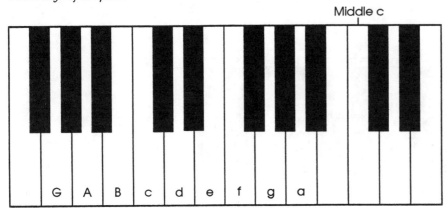

The distances between letter names are not all the same. Of particular importance are the *half-step* intervals found between B and C and between E and F. With the exception of these two white-key combinations or natural half steps, all other staff letter names are spaced at a whole-step interval.

Example 16
The natural half steps.

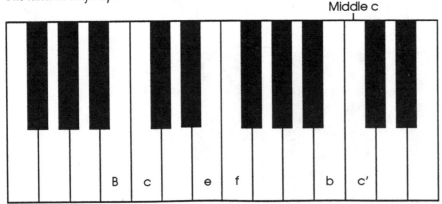

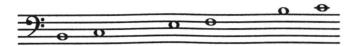

ACCIDENTALS

The tonal arrangement presented up to this point has been a partial study of the keyboard. The keyboard is made up of white keys as well as black keys. The identification or naming of these keys with their **enharmonic** or *alternate names* is brought about by the use of five characters, which are referred to as **accidentals**.

1. The **natural** sign ♮
2. The **sharp** sign ♯
3. The **flat** sign ♭
4. The **double sharp** sign ✗
5. The **double flat** sign ♭♭

All accidentals are placed to the left of each note head they are to affect and are shown on the staff (spaces and lines), as in Example 17.

Example 17
Accidentals.

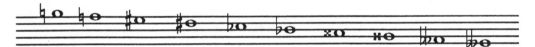

In modern notational practice accidentals are generally governed (exclusive of key signatures) by *eight* **principles of application.**

1. To lower a natural pitch by one half step, use a flat.

Example 18
Use of a flat.

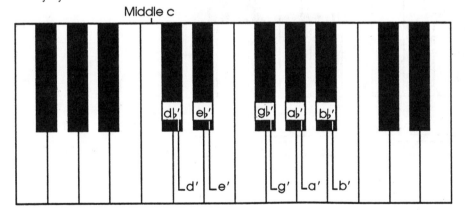

2. To raise a natural pitch by one half step, use a sharp.

Example 19
Use of a sharp.

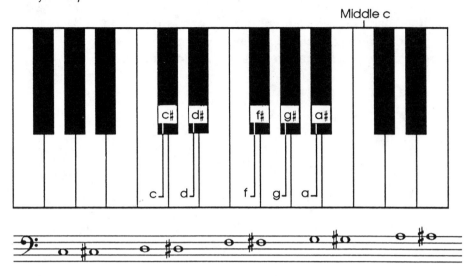

3. To raise a flat pitch by one half step, use a natural.

Example 20
Use of a natural to raise a flat pitch.

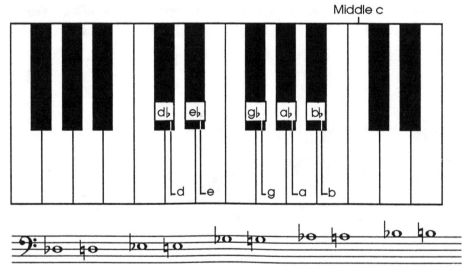

4. To lower a sharp pitch by one half step, use a natural.

Example 21
Use of a natural to lower a sharp pitch.

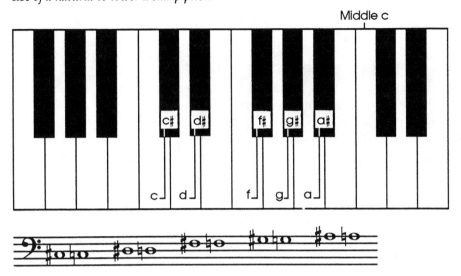

5. To lower a flat pitch by one half step, use a double flat.*

Example 22
Use of a double flat to lower a flat pitch.

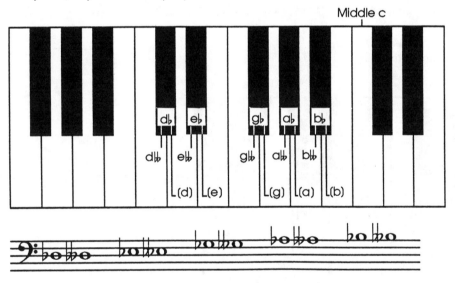

---

*Double flats and double sharps are derived from their natural state. Thus, B♭♭ begins with B and continues through B♭ to A; hence, B♭♭ is exactly the same sound or the enharmonic of A. In similar fashion, G✗ begins with G and continues through G♯ to A; it sounds exactly the same pitch as A and is the enharmonic of A.

6. To raise a double flat by one half step, use a single flat.

Example 23

Use of a single flat to raise a double flat.

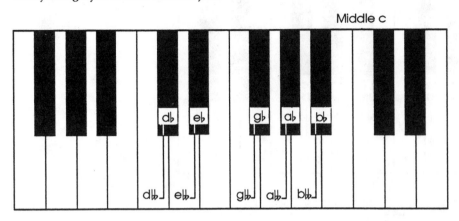

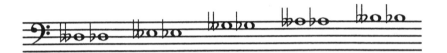

7. To raise a sharp pitch by one half step, use a double sharp.

Example 24

Use of a double sharp to raise a sharp pitch.

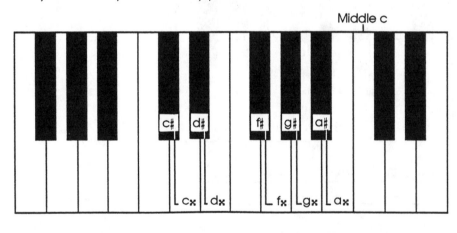

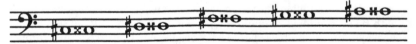

8. To lower a double sharp by one half step, use a single sharp.

Example 25

Use of a single sharp to lower a double sharp.

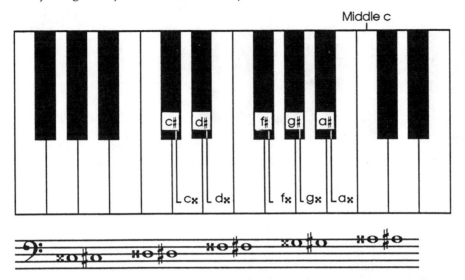

ENHARMONIC CONSIDERATIONS

The tonal arrangement of the keyboard and our present-day system of notation allow for the naming of a single pitch by different names. For example, A may be written as G✖ or B♭♭, and F♯ may be written as G♭. In these cases, the two or more notes representing the same pitch are said to be **enharmonic**. That is to say, G♯ is the enharmonic of A♭, or D♭ is the enharmonic of C♯, and so on. Therefore, by the use of accidentals, each pitch of the tonal arrangement may be indicated in three different ways, with the one exception of the middle black key in the group of three found on the piano keyboard. This pitch may only be shown as G♯ or A♭. These enharmonic considerations are illustrated in Examples 26–31 on pages 31–34.

Example 26

Enharmonic names and pitches.

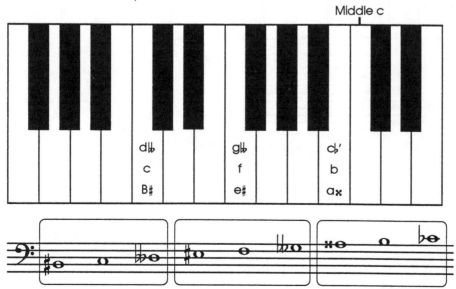

Example 27

Enharmonic names and pitches.

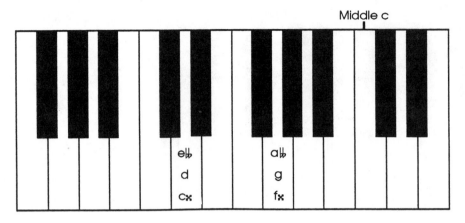

Example 28

Enharmonic names and pitches.

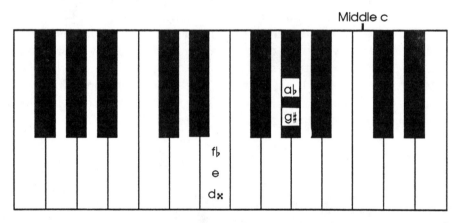

Example 29

Enharmonic names and pitches.

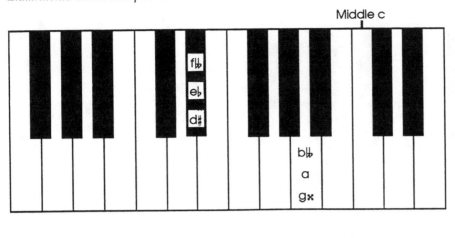

Example 30

Enharmonic names and pitches.

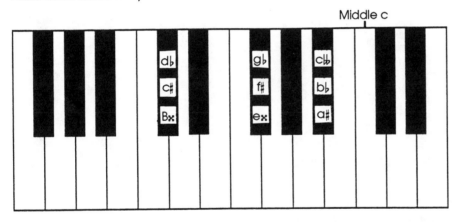

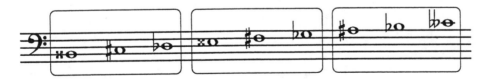

Example 31

The complete letter-name identification of the keyboard.

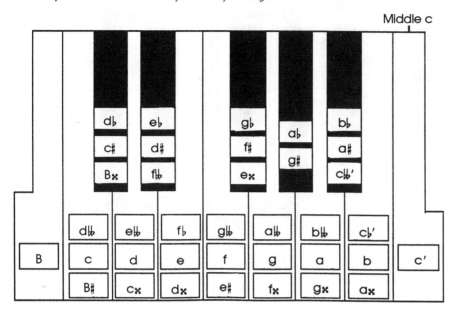

Section

2

The Notation of Rhythm

TIME SIGNATURES

A **time signature** is designed to provide performers with information concerning the **rhythmic** aspects of a composition, that is, the pattern of movement in time. The time signature is given at the beginning of a composition to indicate **meter**, a system of time in which the time signature and bar lines concisely measure and organize rhythmic invention. A time signature appears as a fraction-like representation of two numbers placed one above the other. Although a time signature is *not* to be considered a fraction, the upper number is commonly referred to as the **numerator** and the bottom number as the **denominator**. Two very important pieces of information are to be understood from these numbers.

1. The upper number or *numerator* refers to the number of **beats** (pulses) to be found within a *measure*.

2. The lower number or *denominator* indicates the chosen unit of time or, more specifically, the type of note value that receives the beat or unit of *measure*.

A **measure** is best described as a musical expression that is set between two **bar lines** and that conveys a rhythmic, melodic, or harmonic idea. Additionally, it should be understood that it is possible to have a complete or an incomplete measure at the beginning of a composition with only one bar line. (See Example 32.)

Study the following diagram along with materials presented so far.

Example 32
Elements of meter.

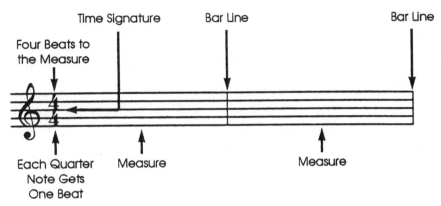

Perhaps, one of the most misunderstood concepts relating to the time signature is the role of note-value equivalencies of the denominator. Note values are represented by numbers. Often this little-known fact prevents the musician from totally understanding the time signature. In order to eliminate this confusion, study the following chart of denominator equivalencies, and memorize each representative number as well as the note value it stands for.

Table 3 ▪ *Denominator Equivalency Chart*			
1 = o		**8** = ♪	
2 = 𝅗𝅥		**16** = ♬	
4 = ♩		(et cetera)	

In order to facilitate what has just been presented, let us examine three different time signatures.

In this time signature, known as **common time**, the *numerator* refers to four (**4**) beats to the measure.

The number four (**4**) in the *denominator* refers to the unit of measure. Additionally, this number also tells us that the unit of measure or the type of note value that receives one beat is the quarter note.

Example 33 is an excerpt of rhythmic design in ⁴⁄₄ time.

Example 33

Rhythm design in ⁴⁄₄ time.

In this time signature, the *numerator* refers to three (**3**) beats to the measure.

The number eight (**8**) in the *denominator* refers to the unit of measure. Additionally, this number also tells us that the unit of measure or the type of note value which receives one beat is the eighth note.

Example 34 is an excerpt of rhythmic design in ³⁄₈ time.

Example 34

Rhythm design in ³⁄₈ time.

In this time signature, the *numerator* refers to two (**2**) pulses or beats to the measure.

The number two (**2**) in the *denominator* refers to the unit of measure. Additionally, this number also tells us that the unit of measure or the type of note value that receives one beat is the half note.

Example 35 is an excerpt of rhythmic design in ²⁄₂ time, also known as **cut time**. Notice that, visually, each measure of ²⁄₂ time appears to contain the same number of beats as in ⁴⁄₄ time. The differences between the excerpts (Examples 33 and 35) are the time signatures and the intended modes of performance.

Example 35

Rhythm design in ²⁄₂ time.

MANUSCRIPT TIPS

Although a clef sign must be placed on each successive staff of a complete page of a score, it is customary to place a *time signature* only at the beginning of a composition and only on the *first staff*. Occasionally in compositions, a time signature may change; when this takes place, the new time signature must be placed at the point of change. When writing on staff paper, time signatures are never to be written with a horizontal line between the numerator and the denominator. Additional information concerning time signatures will be found in later chapters.

Manuscript Practice

Use these manuscript pages for note taking and drill.

DRILL STUDY #1

Instructions: Using sharps or flats, place one *enharmonic* equivalent to the right of each given pitch, and supply the exact letter name in the brackets provided below each measure. In addition, use *half notes* for the entire study; be sure to place the stems in the right direction. Use the first (screened) measure of Exercise 1 as a model for Exercises 1–5.

1.

(f#′ / g♭′) (d#″/   ) (a#′/   ) (c#″/   ) (g#′/   ) (d#′/   )

2.

(d♭″/   ) (a♭′/   ) (g♭″/   ) (b♭′/   ) (e♭″/   ) (g♭′/   )

3.

(d♭′/   ) (a♭″/   ) (e♭′/   ) (b♭″/   ) (d♭‴/   ) (e♭‴/   )

4.
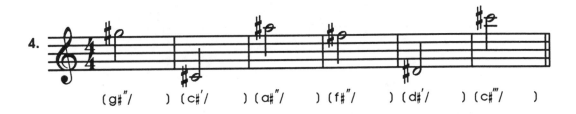

(g#″/   ) (c#′/   ) (a#″/   ) (f#″/   ) (d#′/   ) (c#‴/   )

5.

(g♭″/   ) (a#′/   ) (d♭″/   ) (g#″/   ) (a♭′/   ) (f#′/   )

Instructions: Exercises 6 and 7 relate to enharmonic tones that are neither sharp nor flat. Place an enharmonic pitch to the right of each given pitch and supply its exact letter name in the bracket provided. Make sure to place your stems in the right direction.

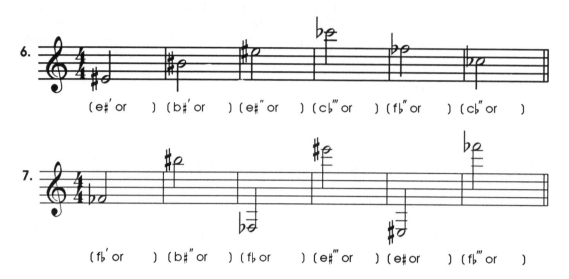

Instructions: In Exercises 8 and 9, by utilizing accidentals, raise each pitch by one half step. Refer to the chapter as often as is necessary to make sure that each response is correct.

Instructions: In Exercise 10, use the double-sharp sign to raise each pitch one half step.

DRILL STUDY #2

Instructions: In Exercises 1–6, by utilizing the appropriate accidentals, lower each given pitch by one half step. In addition, use *eighth notes* for the entire study; be sure to place the stems and flags in the right directions. Refer to the chapter as often as is necessary to ensure the correct responses. Use the first two (screened) measures of Exercise 1 as a model for Exercises 1–6.

Instructions: For Exercises 7–10: Utilizing all possible accidentals, place one enharmonic equivalent along with the proper note value, according to the time signature, on either side of each given pitch. In addition, supply the exact letter name within the brackets provided below each staff.

7.   (/ a' /   ) (/ d" /   ) (/ g' /   )

8.   (/ c' /   ) (/ f♯ /   ) (/ b♭ /   )

9.   (/ c♯' /   ) (/ e♭ /   ) (/ a /   )

10.   (/ f /   ) (/ E /   ) (/ B /   )

Instructions: In Exercises 11 and 12, only one enharmonic equivalent is possible. Place this pitch to the right of each given note, supply the exact letter name within the bracket provided, and choose the proper note value to complete each measure according to the time signature.

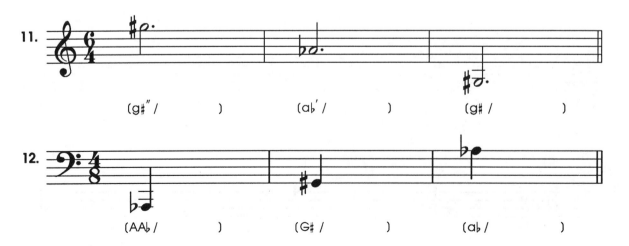

11.   (g♯" /   ) (a♭' /   ) (g♯ /   )

12.   (AA♭ /   ) (G♯ /   ) (a♭ /   )

ASSIGNMENT FOR CHAPTER 2

NAME _____ SCORE _____ GRADE _____

DATE DUE _____ SECTION _____ INSTRUCTOR _____

1. *Instructions:* In Parts (a)–(d), using the appropriate pitches, place one enharmonic equivalent on each side of the given pitch and give the exact letter name for each pitch within the brackets provided immediately below each measure. In addition, be sure to select the appropriate note values, according to the time signature, to ensure complete measures of music.

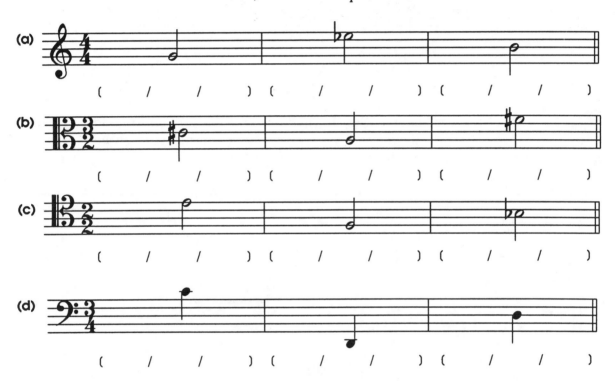

2. *Instructions:* In Parts (a) and (b), use the same instructions to Exercise 1, but with one exception. Place two enharmonic equivalents to the *right* of the given pitch and be sure to select the proper note values, according to the time signature, to ensure complete measures of music.

3. **Instructions:** In Parts (a) and (b), use the same instructions as in Exercise 1, but with one exception. Place two enharmonic equivalents to the *left* of the given pitch and be sure to select the proper note values, according to the time signature, to ensure complete measures of music.

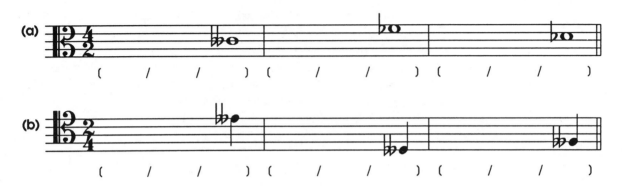

4. **Instructions:** In rhythmic excerpts (a) and (d), add bar lines to divide the rhythmic note values correctly, according to the time signature.

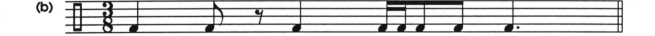

---

*This utilizes a modern clef sign used by contemporary composers who are concerned only with rhythm when writing for unpitched percussion instruments. Treble and bass clef signs are usually reserved for pitched percussion instruments.

CHAPTER

3

CHROMATIC
SCALES
and
RHYTHM

Section

1

Pitch Considerations

THE CHROMATIC SCALE

Music of our Western civilization is based upon an organizational system of pitches, collectively referred to as **scales**. This scale system, which acts as a reservoir of pitches for *melodic* and/or *harmonic* invention, is the lifeblood of the composer's art.

The primary and most basic scale of this system is the **chromatic** or **twelve tone (12-tone) scale**. It is a scale that reflects a specific structure involving the use of half steps. By placing successive pitches one half step apart within one octave and then repeating the starting pitch one octave higher, a scale of thirteen pitches emerges. It should be understood that although thirteen pitches are shown in the writing of the scale, chromatic scales divide the octave into twelve (12) equal half steps (**degrees**). The thirteenth pitch is merely the restatement of the starting pitch one octave higher. It should be further understood that chromatic scales can be started on any degree of the piano keyboard.

In Examples 36 and 37, carefully compare each ascending and descending scale pattern presented and note the unusual use of *flats ascending* and *sharps descending*, as well as the mixture of the two. Although this notation is used and is considered grammatically correct, it is preferable, however, to use *sharps ascending* and *flats descending*, as presented in Example 37. The underlying factor is the consideration of "tendency tones" and their direction of resolution; e.g., D♯ to E, A♯ to B, G♭ to F, A♭ to G, and so forth.

Example 36
Flats and naturals ascending and sharps and naturals descending.

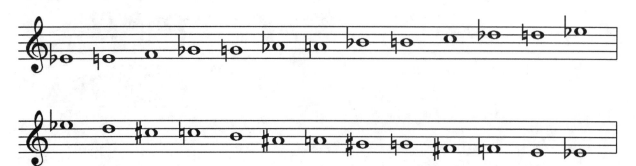

Example 37

Sharps ascending and flats descending.

For the sake of consistency and for avoiding complications when notating chromatic scales, it is always wise to observe the natural half steps between B and C as well as between E and F. Carefully study the following excerpts taken from actual written chromatic passages. Chromatic lines are identified by brackets.

Example 38

Examples of chromatic use.

Johann Sebastian Bach, *Chromatic Fantasie and Fugue*, "Fugue Theme," Measures 1–6.

Ernest Bloch, *Concerto Grosso for String Orchestra and Piano*, "Obbligato," 2nd Movement, 2nd Theme, Measures 1–4.

Ludwig Van Beethoven, *Sonata No. 2 in A*, Opus 2, No. 2 for Piano, 4th Movement, 2nd Theme, Measures 1–2.

To conclude the study of chromatic scales, let us review and finalize some very important points.

1. All chromatic scales span the architectural limits of an octave.

2. All chromatic scales are constructed with pitches that are placed one half step apart.

3. All chromatic scales repeat their starting pitches one octave above or below, depending on the direction of the scale.

4. All chromatic scales are based upon the half-step principle, which asserts that the octave is divided into twelve (12) equal half steps.

5. In the notating of chromatic scales, it is preferable to utilize sharps ascending and flats descending.

6. It is always wise to observe the natural half steps between B and C as well as between E and F in the notating of chromatic scales.

Section

2

The Notation of Rhythm

THE METRONOME

Tempo refers to the measurement of speed of a musical composition. In the hands of the composer, conductor, or performer, it is often a very difficult aspect of music to control. Fortunately, Johann Nepomuk Maelzel, a German of the early nineteenth century, invented a device called a **metronome** that produces 40 to 208 regular ticks per minute. This device indicates the speed of a musical composition to the composer, conductor, or performer. It works in the following manner: If one were to set the metronome at 60 beats per minute with a quarter note being the unit of measure or pulse, there would be 60 quarter notes per minute; if the unit of measure is a half note, there would be 60 half notes—or 120 quarter notes—each minute.

Although the metronome is accurate and exacting, metronome markings are seldom the only means of indicating the tempo of a musical composition. Most compositions usually have a descriptive term placed at the beginning—generally in Italian, the international language of music, or in other languages, such as French, German, or even English. Language indicators are relative and, for the most part, subjective. Thus, when an arranger or composer combines the descriptive indicators of language and the exacting tempo settings of a metronome, the speed of a composition is both accurately and subjectively set for the performer. More information on the placement of metronome markings and language indicators will be presented in this chapter in the *Manuscript Tips* section. Additional information on various other metronome markings and language indicators will be given in forthcoming chapters.

ABBREVIATED TIME SIGNATURES

Abbreviated time signatures are often seen in the notation of rhythm. They appear as symbols in place of numbered time signatures. One symbol that appears quite frequently is **c**, which designates the time signature $\frac{4}{4}$, or *common time*. Another widely used symbol is **¢**, which indicates $\frac{2}{2}$, or *cut time*. As can clearly be seen, this symbol is drawn with a vertical line bisecting the **c** in order to represent, literally, a halving of the quadruple time signature, thereby producing $\frac{2}{2}$ time. It is important to understand that *two/two* is half of *four/four* in the number of beats per measure, although the same number of quarter notes would appear in a measure of music of both meters. The most important difference between these two meters is felt in the performance of the natural accents per measure.

The following example presents a comparative analysis of both meters and their abbreviated substitute time signatures. Pay particular attention to the metronome markings, which are written above the time signatures, **downbeat** (accented beat) and **upbeat** (unaccented beat) arrows, and beats per measure.

Example 39
The comparison of common time and cut time.

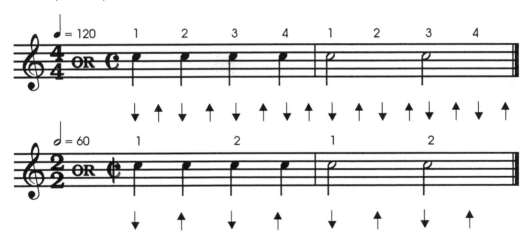

MANUSCRIPT TIPS

The placement of a metronome marking and/or a descriptive language term is essential for the performance of a composition. When both performance directions are given, they are placed at the beginning of a composition above the uppermost staff—well above flags, stems, and other notational symbols—or at other appropriate points in the body of the composition. The first letter of the descriptive language term (usually in upper case) is customarily aligned over the time signature, while the metronome marking (sometimes enclosed in parentheses in older music) is placed immediately to the right of the descriptive term and together they are shown as:

Andante ♩ = 60

Not all performance directions are given in pairs. Often, a descriptive term is used by itself. A metronome marking can also exist without a descriptive language term, in which case it may be seen with an abbreviated expression, such as M. M. = 60. This expression is aligned in the same fashion as a descriptive term and, as we have seen before, merely instructs the performer to set the **Maelzel's Metronome** to sixty (60) ticks per minute.* Finally, performance directions may be given in pairs, one above the other, as in the body of a composition and may also include an abbreviation in the expression

♩ = ca. 60

This abbreviation stands for "circa" and indicates that the composition is to be played at *about* 60 quarter notes per minute—give or take a few beats, one way or the other.

The following example provides most of the commonly used placements and alignments for

(a) combined language descriptive terms and metronome markings,

(b) language descriptive terms only,

(c) metronome markings only, and

(d) and (e) different combinations that may be placed in the body of the composition.

Example 40

Commonly used placements and alignments.

---

*M. M. is derived from "Maelzel's Metronome," and *not* from "metronome marking."

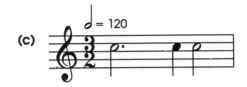

(c)

(d)

(e)

Lento = Slow
Moderato = Moderate
Allegro = Fast

A SUGGESTED METHOD OF STUDY

Every effort should be made to parallel the learning process of writing spatial distances with the development of one's ear. Therefore, from this point on, it is imperative that each student play each exercise on the piano, and whenever possible, on any other instrument he or she may know, in order to appreciate both visually and aurally the various combinations of spatial distances to be learned. It is equally important to develop the ability to sing each and every type of scale, interval, and chord introduced. In this regard, the moveable "do" system, solfeggio, numbers, or letter names of pitches may be used for this purpose. Whenever singing or playing these exercises on a string or wind instrument, pay close attention to the principles of good intonation. The ability to hear, play, and sing in tune is of paramount importance to the performing musician.

Manuscript Practice

Use these manuscript pages for note taking and drill.

DRILL STUDY #1

Instructions: In Exercises 1–6, utilizing sharps ascending and flats descending, place the missing pitches under the designated markers (ˈ) to form chromatic scale segments. These equally spaced markers are provided to ensure good manuscript habits. In addition, supply the proper note values according to the time signatures, and *play* each exercise in accordance with the performance indicators given in the upper left-hand corner.

Instructions: In Exercises 7 and 8, additional practice on the notating of natural half steps is provided. Place the missing chromatic pitches under the designated markers. Do these carefully and refer to the chapter as often as is necessary. Pay close attention to time signatures, performance directions, correct note values, and good manuscript.

Instructions: In Exercises 9–12, utilizing flat and natural signs ascending and sharp and natural signs descending, place the missing chromatic pitches under the designated markers. Because of the complexities of writing these segments, check your results carefully.

DRILL STUDY #2

Instructions: In Exercises 1–6, utilizing sharps ascending and flats descending, place the missing chromatic pitches under the designated markers. The natural half steps between B and C as well as between E and F have already been supplied in each chromatic scale. In addition, supply the proper note values according to the time signatures and *play* each exercise in accordance with the performance indicators given.

Instructions: In Exercise 7, utilize flat and natural signs ascending and in Exercise No. 8, utilize sharp and natural signs descending. Place the missing chromatic pitches under the designated markers. Again, because of the complexity of writing these chromatic scales, check your results carefully. When completed, *play* each exercise in accordance with the performance indicators given.

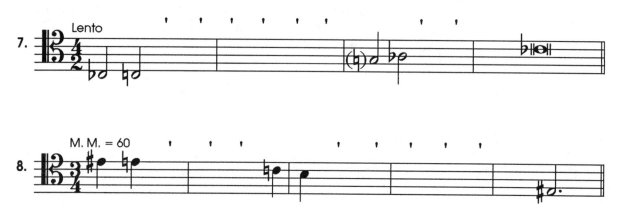

Instructions: Although chromatic scales are ideally written with sharps ascending and flats descending, examples exist in various works of the musical literature of sharps and flats intermingled within the same scale. Place the missing chromatic pitches under the designated markers. Any order of sharps or flats will be acceptable in completing the chromatic scales in Exercises 9–12.

ASSIGNMENT FOR CHAPTER 3

NAME _____ SCORE _____ GRADE _____

DATE DUE _____ SECTION _____ INSTRUCTOR _____

Instructions: In Parts (a)–(l), utilizing sharps ascending and flats descending, place the missing pitches under the designated markers within each given chromatic scale. Observe the spacing markers to ensure proper manuscript notation. When completed, *play* each of these exercises in accordance with the performance indicators given.

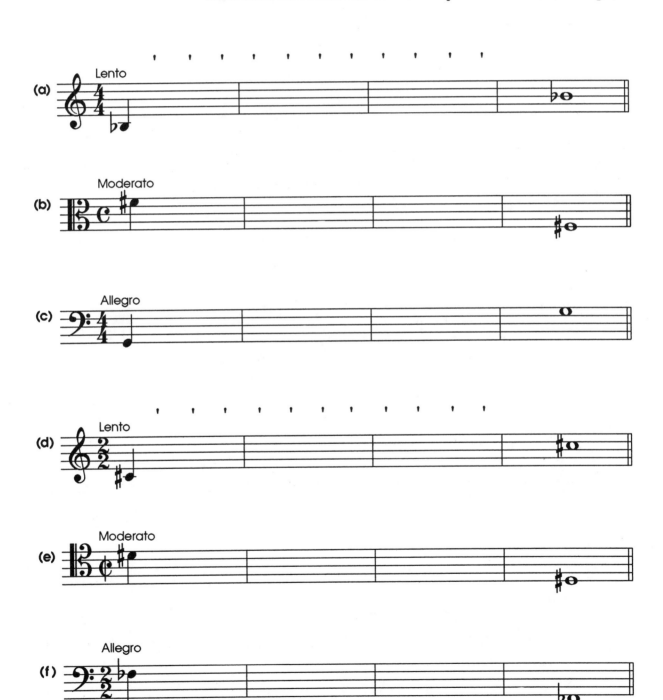

(g) M. M. = ca. 50

(h) M. M. = ca. 84

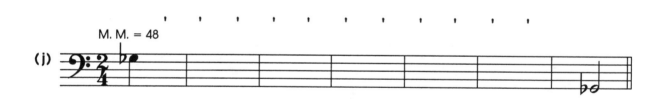

(i) M. M. = 126

(j) M. M. = 48

(k) M. M. = 100

(l) M. M. = ca 132

PERFORMANCE ASSIGNMENT FOR CHAPTER 3

Instructions: The graded exercises in Parts (a)–(c) are meant to be used as an additional or optional assignment. These challenging, performance-oriented exercises are designed to monitor progress, understanding, and comprehension of the materials presented. By adjusting octave ranges and/or clefs, it is possible to perform these exercises on various instruments; however, the recommended instrument is the piano. See the list, *Performance Terms and Expression Marks* on pages 257–60.

Suggested Chromatic Fingerings for the Piano Keyboard

Right Hand [R. H.] When playing the natural half-step combinations (B&C/E&F), the lower notes (B&E) will be played with the thumb, which we will designate as ❶. The index finger, which we will designate as ❷, will play the upper notes (C&F). The middle finger, which we will designate as ❸, will play all the black keys, while the thumb (❶) will play all the remaining white keys. Thus, a chromatic scale (ascending or descending) from e' to e" will use the following fingerings: ❶❷❸❶❸❶❸❶❷❸❶❸❶.

Left Hand [L. H.] When playing the natural half-step combinations (B&C/E&F), the upper notes (C&F) will be played with the thumb, which we will designate as ❶. The index finger, which we will designate as ❷, will play the lower notes (B&E). The middle finger, which we will designate as ❸, will play all the black keys, while the thumb (❶) will play all the remaining white keys. Thus, a chromatic scale (ascending or descending) from e' to e will use the following fingerings: ❷❶❸❶❸❶❸❷❶❸❶❸❷.

Level I

Level II

Level III

CHAPTER

4

MODAL
SCALES
and
RHYTHM

Section

1

Pitch Considerations

MODAL SCALES

Music of the twentieth century has borrowed heavily from the past. In today's popular music, the borrowing of earlier techniques of composition is quite common among rock performers, commercial musicians, and improvisors of modern jazz. Even celebrated and classically oriented contemporary composers have used melodic concepts taken from prebaroque eras and have combined them with modern harmonic and melodic techniques to create fresh and "new" viable sounds. One of the most commonly borrowed systems is a series of scales called **modes.**

Because of their past religious usage, **modal scales** are referred to as **church** or **ecclesiastical modes.** They predate the inception of the *major* and *minor system* of the seventeenth century and form the necessary reservoir of tones for the seven modes to be discussed in this chapter.

Each of the natural pitches of the musical alphabet forms a basis for the scale and the starting **tone** (pitch) for each of the seven modes. The modal and letter names of these scales are given in Table 4.

Historically, the **Dorian, Phrygian, Lydian,** and **Mixolydian modes** are placed about the eighth century, whereas the **Ionian** and **Aeolian modes** were not introduced until the seventeenth century. The **Locrian mode,** which was felt to be lacking in tonality, existed only as a theoretical possibility and as such, was rarely used.

In Example 41 careful attention should be given to the half-step pattern of each mode presented.

Table 4 ■ *Modal and Letter Names*							
MODAL NAMES	**SCALE LETTER NAMES**						
Aeolian	A	B	C	D	E	F	G	A
Locrian	B	C	D	E	F	G	A	B
Ionian	C	D	E	F	G	A	B	C
Dorian	D	E	F	G	A	B	C	D
Phrygian	E	F	G	A	B	C	D	E
Lydian	F	G	A	B	C	D	E	F
Mixolydian	G	A	B	C	D	E	F	G

Example 41
Modal scales.

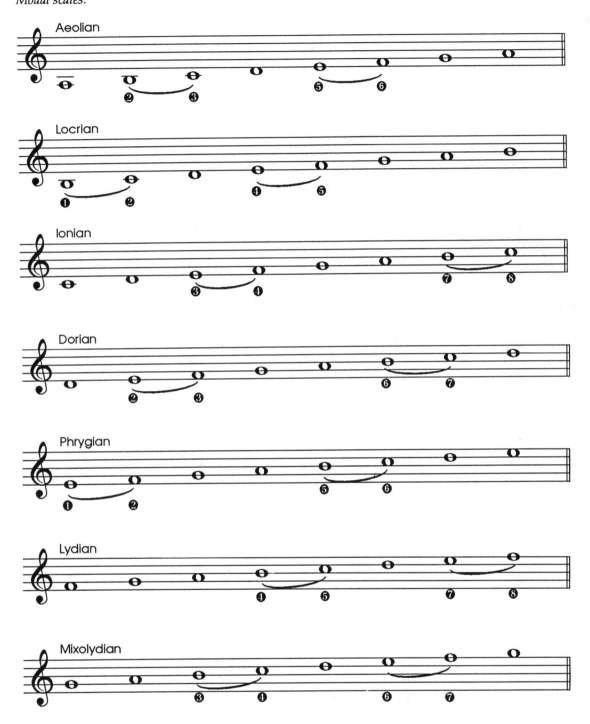

Transposition, or the moving of melodic or harmonic patterns to other **scale degrees** (scale steps) of the keyboard, is a very important technique to learn. It is a method similar to one which might be employed by a garment manufacturer who produces many different-colored dresses but, always, from the same pattern. In the transposing of modes, one merely observes the proper half-step pattern and supplies the necessary accidentals to the particular mode or modes intended. In the following example, the *Dorian mode*

has been constructed on three different pitches. From the very onset, it is important to know that the Dorian mode has half steps between the 2nd and 3rd, as well as between the 6th and 7th degrees; all other intervals are a whole step apart. By this method of careful calculation and analysis, transposition of all modes is possible.

Example 42

Transposed Dorians.

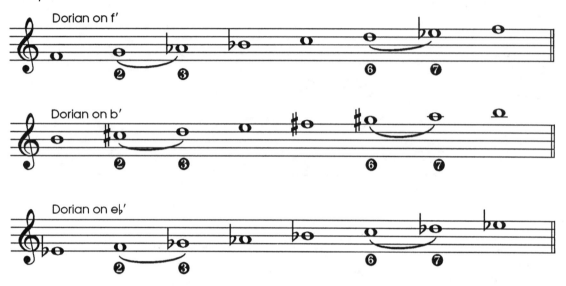

MODAL-SCALE SYNTHESIS

All modal scales can be reduced essentially to combinations of four basic **tetrachords**, which are series of four-note segments, with four different intervallic structures.

The *four tetrachord patterns* are as follows:

1. Tetrachord No. 1 [*W-W-H*] contains two successive whole steps and a half step.

2. Tetrachord No. 2 [*W-H-W*] contains one whole step followed by a half step and another whole step.

3. Tetrachord No. 3 [*H-W-W*] contains one half step followed by two successive whole steps.

4. Tetrachord No. 4 [*W-W-W*] contains three successive whole steps.

When two of the above tetrachords are placed one after another in succession and in a specific order, a mode is derived. For instance, the combination of two No. 1 tetrachords in succession yields the Ionian mode. The combination of Tetrachord No. 1 followed by Tetrachord No. 2 yields the Mixolydian mode. By continuing this process, Table 5 can be realized.

Finally, the interval between two successive tetrachords may be a half step or a whole step, depending upon which two tetrachords are being combined. The Lydian and Locrian use the half-step hookup between tetrachords, while all others use a whole step.

Table 5 ▪ *Four Modal Tetrachord Patterns*

Tetrachord No. 1

(W–W–H)

Tetrachord No. 2

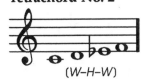

(W–H–W)

Tetrachord No. 3

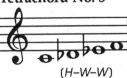

(H–W–W)

Tetrachord No. 4

(W–W–W)

For the purposes of formulating this chart, each tetrachord has been placed on *middle c*; any other keynote could have served the same purpose.

▪ ▪ ▪

Ionian mode = Two successive No. 1 Tetrachords
For example: D Ionian = DEF♯G   ABC♯D

Dorian mode = Two successive No. 2 Tetrachords
For example: G Dorian = GAB♭C   DEFG

Phrygian mode = Two successive No. 3 Tetrachords
For example: B Phrygian = BCDE   F♯GAB

Lydian mode = Tetrachord No. 4 followed by Tetrachord No. 1
For example: E Lydian = EF♯G♯A♯   BC♯D♯E

Mixolydian mode = Tetrachord No. 1 followed by Tetrachord No. 2
For example: F Mixolydian = FGAB♭   CDE♭F

Aeolian mode = Tetrachord No. 2 followed by Tetrachord No. 3
For example: C Aeolian = CDE♭F   GA♭B♭C

Locrian mode = Tetrachord No. 3 followed by Tetrachord No. 4
For example: A Locrian = AB♭CD   E♭FGA

Before proceeding further, let us review some of the more salient points concerning modes.

1. All modal scales are written within the architectural limits of one octave. Be sure to place the scale degrees on alternating lines and spaces.

2. Each of the seven modes introduced can be constructed from any degree of the keyboard.

3. No two modes have the same half-step pattern.

4. Each mode can be transposed to any note of the keyboard, provided that the same relative half-step pattern for the given mode is observed.

5. All modes can be reduced to four basic tetrachords. When these tetrachords are used in various combinations and in proper succession, they formulate seven modal scales. In addition, all descending tetrachord patterns *must* sound the same as their corresponding ascending patterns. Therefore, Tetrachord patterns No. 1 [*W-W-H/H-W-W*] and No. 3 [*H-W-W/W-W-H*] must be reversed in order to achieve the same notes and the same sounds when ascending and descending. Tetrachord patterns No. 2 [*W-H-W/W-H-W*] and No. 4 [*W-W-W/W-W-W*] present no problems because they remain consistent whether they are ascending or descending.

6. All accidentals are to be placed within the scale and on the particular degrees to be affected, and neither in a group nor singularly before the scale.

7. The two modes that begin with the letter "L" (the *Lydian* and *Locrian*) use a half-step hookup between the successive tetrachords, while all others use a whole step.

8. Finally, the memorization of mode order is very important and can be extremely helpful in working with modes. Using association and imagination as basic memory ingredients, the following (ungrammatical) sentence will help in the memorization process.

> **All's** (*Aeolian*) **lost** (*Locrian*), **if** (*Ionian*) **Dori** (*Dorian*) **plays** (*Phrygian*) **like** (*Lydian*) **me** (*Mixolydian*).

Section

2

The Notation of Rhythm

REVIEW OF BASIC CONCEPTS

Before presenting new materials on rhythm, let us review some important concepts. Composers, arrangers, and performers use *note values* to symbolize lengths or durations of time and *rest* symbols to represent durations of silence. *Flags*, as they relate to note values and assorted rests, provide the necessary means to shorten set durations of time. *Dots* and *ties* lengthen time. *Metronome markings* and *descriptive language terms* indicate tempo settings. *Meter* is a system of time in which time signatures and bar lines concisely measure and organize rhythmic invention. Finally, with all these component parts in place, the writing of music and, specifically, its rhythmical aspect, is made clear, concise, and meaningful to the composer, arranger, and performer.

SIMPLE TIME

Additional information on time signatures is needed to understand fully the importance of meter. Specifically, time signatures relate directly to the division of the beat. When the beat is divided into two equal parts, the time signature is in **simple time**, or **simple meter**. These simple-time signatures clearly represent what they purport to say. As the following time signature indicates, two/four $\left(\frac{2}{4}\right)$ time (meter) contains two beats to the measure, and the unit of measure is a quarter note.

Simple-time signatures are found in three separate categories; they can be classified as **simple duple** (meaning two beats to the measure), **simple triple** (meaning three beats to the measure), or **simple quadruple** (meaning four beats to the measure). Time signatures beyond four that are not multiple extensions of simple time are either *compound* or *asymmetrical*. Although the concept of compound time will be dealt with in forthcoming chapters, asymmetrical time is beyond the scope of this book and will not be discussed. Table 6 presents most of the possible common time signatures found in simple time.

EQUAL DIVISION

Equal division, which is related directly to time signatures, is one of the most important concepts in the notation of rhythm. It is a concept that governs the notation of **beams** (the use of thick horizontal lines to join stems in note-value groupings) in vocal and instrumental music, the principles of proper grouping, and the act of consolidation. While various parts of the total concept are adaptable to

Table 6 • *Simple-Time Categories*

SIMPLE DUPLE

$\frac{2}{1}$	$\frac{2}{2}$	$\frac{2}{4}$	$\frac{2}{8}$	$\frac{2}{16}$	$\frac{2}{32}$	$\frac{2}{64}$

SIMPLE TRIPLE

$\frac{3}{1}$	$\frac{3}{2}$	$\frac{3}{4}$	$\frac{3}{8}$	$\frac{3}{16}$	$\frac{3}{32}$	$\frac{3}{64}$

SIMPLE QUADRUPLE

$\frac{4}{1}$	$\frac{4}{2}$	$\frac{4}{4}$	$\frac{4}{8}$	$\frac{4}{16}$	$\frac{4}{32}$	$\frac{4}{64}$

simple duple, simple triple, and other meters we have yet to encounter, it is a concept which, in the main, is relegated to quadruple-time signatures.

THE SPLIT

To define the principle of **equal division** clearly, one merely makes certain that the first part of the third beat of each measure is shown as a separate note or rest value or as a tied note value. This ensures the **splitting** of four pulses (beats) into two equal parts within a quadruple environment. The use of the tie between the upbeat of beat two and the downbeat of beat three is permitted. Beams, most often, are *not* permitted; however, certain exceptions do exist with esoteric time signatures that use extremely short unit note values. Study Example 43 as to the placement of the so-called **split** and the ensuing two-part example (Example 44), in which the poorly written top measure is presented along with the correctly written bottom measure of the same intended sound.

The incorrect version given in Example 44 tends to obscure the second, third, and fourth beats of the measure because equal division was not observed. However, the correct version, in which the split was identified and hence, equal division was observed, is easier to read and is no longer rhythmically confusing.

Example 43
The imaginary split.

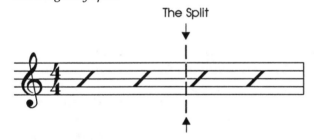

Example 44
Correct and incorrect versions of equal division.

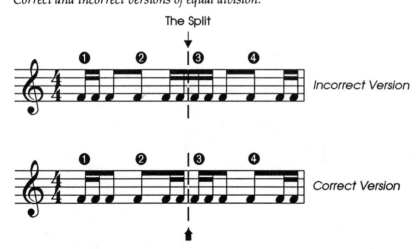

MANUSCRIPT TIPS

Notational rules governing manuscript (handwritten music as opposed to printed music) as it concerns flags and beams are often misunderstood by musicians.

BEAMS

The Notation of Beams in Vocal and Instrumental Music. Individually flagged note values are used in vocal music and are governed, primarily, by **syllabication** (the division of lyrics into syllables). In the last decade or so, publishers of vocal music have incorporated more extensive use of beaming, but for the most part, composers and arrangers dealing with text generally use fewer beams. Instrumental writers, however, who do not use text as a musical ingredient, use beaming techniques exclusively. Study the following comparative measures which concern vocal and instrumental notation.

Example 45
A comparison of vocal and instrumental notation.

Giacomo Puccini, *Tosca*, Act I, Andante Mosso, Measures 2–3, sung by the tenor character, Mario Cavaradossi

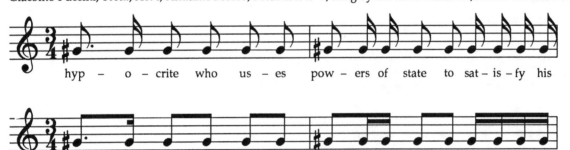

Principles of Proper Grouping. In general, when connecting note heads with beams on either side of the split, it is wise to observe the integrity of each beat. In simple-duple or simple-quadruple time, do not attempt to place beams across beats but, instead, treat each individual beat with its own separate beam to form proper grouping. In the next example, the bottom measure is the correct version.

Example 46
A comparison of proper and improper grouping in simple time.

In cut time a certain degree of flexibility exists. Beats on either side of the split may be connected or disconnected by beams, provided the shortest note value is an eighth note.

Example 47
Acceptable versions in cut time.

If the duration of note values on either side of the split in a duple time signature includes sixteenth notes or notes of shorter duration, it is best to think of the measure as being simply quadruple. This will limit the beaming and preserve proper grouping. In the next example, note the differences between the top and bottom measures. The bottom measure is the preferred written version of the intended sound.

Example 48
Preferred note-value grouping.

Preferred Version

The Act of Consolidation. The **consolidating** or placement of rhythmic elements into beat groupings helps to eliminate clutter. If ties, beams, note heads, and stems can be rearranged to provide better visual acuity, parts of beats can then be combined to cause a higher readability level and thus, provide for better comprehension and for greater success of performance.

Example 49
Consolidation.

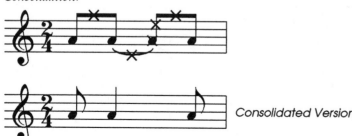

Consolidated Version

In Example 49, two beams, one stem, one note head, and, most importantly, one tie have been eliminated. Although beginning musicians might consider the top measure, with each beat clearly shown, to be much clearer to read, composers, arrangers, and performers would feel that the bottom measure is an improvement over the cluttered upper measure and thus is the measure of choice. Finally, beat groupings that contain sixteenth notes and/or notes of faster duration need *not* be consolidated. Peruse the various parts of Example 50, paying careful attention to each comparative measure—especially, to the optional methods of consolidation for beat groups that contain sixteenth notes and/or notes of shorter duration.

Example 50

Comparative measures of consolidation.

Manuscript Practice

Use these manuscript pages for note taking and drill.

DRILL STUDY #1

Instructions: Within the tetrachord limits provided in Exercises 1–4, place the missing second and third notes of *tetrachord pattern No. 1,* shown below. Be sure to alternate lines and spaces and to place each missing note directly under the spacing markers provided to ensure good manuscript. It should be understood that descending tetrachords sound the same as their corresponding ascending patterns. Play and listen carefully to each tetrachord on the piano.

Tetrachord No. 1 – [*W-W-H*]

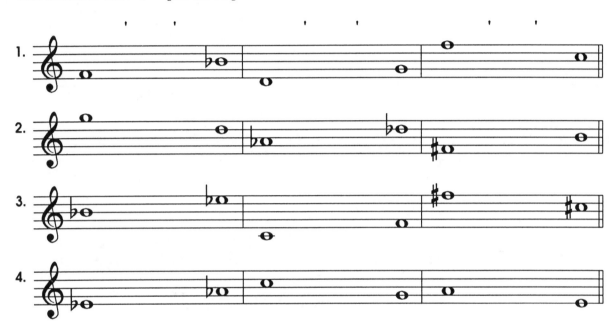

Instructions: Using the instructions to Exercises 1–4, substitute *tetrachord pattern No. 2* in Exercises 5–7.

Tetrachord No. 2 – [*W-H-W*]

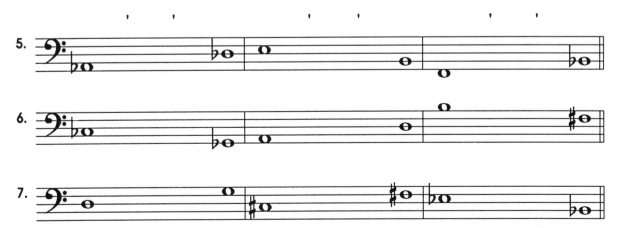

Instructions: Using the instructions to Exercises 1–4, substitute *tetrachord pattern No. 3* in Exercises 8–11.

Tetrachord No. 3 – [*H-W-W*]

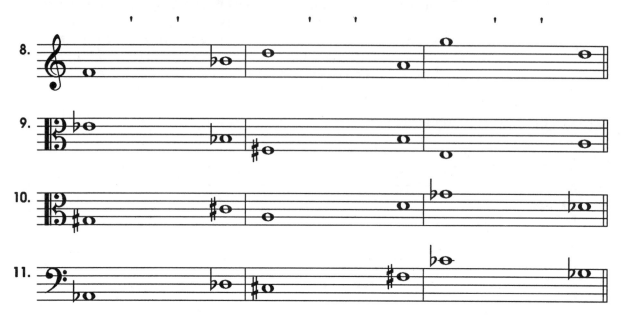

Instructions: In Exercises 12–15, using *tetrachord pattern No. 4*, supply all of the missing notes directly under the spacing markers in ascending fashion. Be sure to alternate lines and spaces and to place each note head directly under the spacing markers provided.

Tetrachord No. 4 – [*W-W-W*]

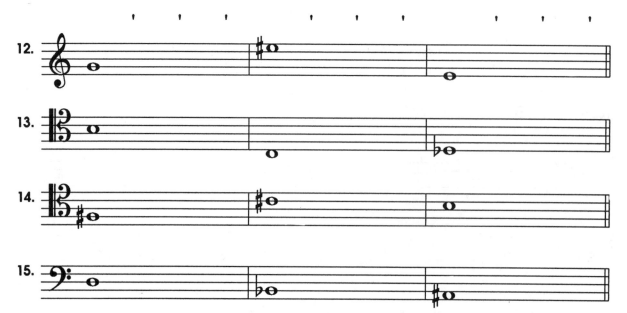

DRILL STUDY #2

Instructions: By combining two successive *No. 1 tetrachord patterns,* supply the missing notes to the *Ionian modes* given in Exercises 1–3. Be sure to alternate lines and spaces and to place each missing note directly under the spacing marker provided. In addition, supply each proper note value in accordance with the time signature and play or sing each completed modal form.

Ionian mode – No. 1 [*W-W-H*] / No. 1 [*W-W-H*]

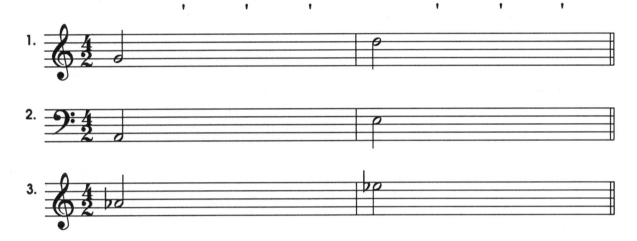

Instructions: Substitute the *Dorian mode* in Exercises 4–6 and proceed as indicated in the instructions to Exercises 1–3.

Dorian mode – No. 2 [*W-H-W*] / No. 2 [*W-H-W*]

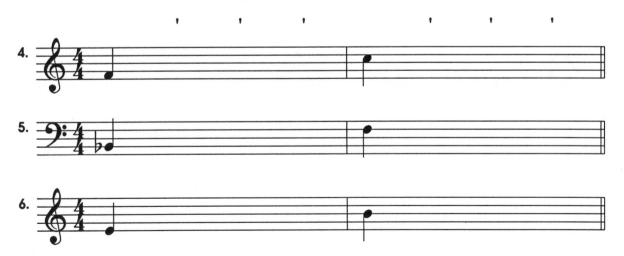

Instructions: Substitute the *Phrygian mode* in Exercises 7–9 and proceed as indicated in the instructions to Exercises 1–3.

Phrygian mode – No. 3 [*H-W-W*] / No. 3 [*H-W-W*]

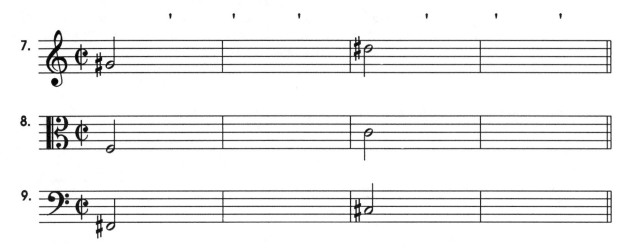

Instructions: Substitute the *Lydian mode* in Exercises 10–12 and proceed as indicated in the instructions to Exercises 1–3.

Lydian mode – No. 4 [*W-W-W*] / No. 1 [*W-W-H*]

DRILL STUDY #3

Instructions: In Exercises 1–3, by combining a *No. 1 tetrachord pattern* followed by a *No. 2 tetrachord pattern*, supply the missing notes to the *Mixolydian mode*. Be sure to alternate lines and spaces and to place each missing note directly under the spacing markers provided. In addition, supply each proper note value in accordance with the time signature and play or sing each complete modal form.

Mixolydian mode – No. 1 [*W-W-H*] / No. 2 [*W-H-W*]

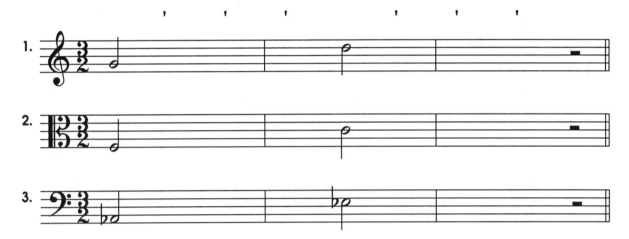

Instructions: Substitute the *Aeolian mode* in Exercises 4–6 and proceed as indicated in the instructions to Exercises 1–3.

Aeolian mode – No. 2 [*W-H-W*] / No. 3 [*H-W-W*]

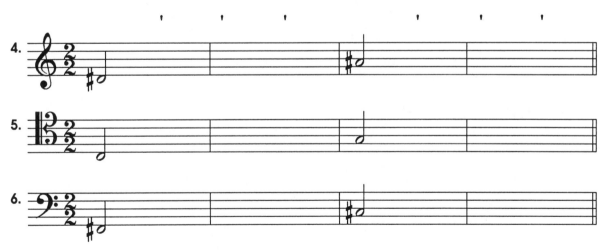

Instructions: Substitute the *Locrian mode* in Exercises 7–9 and proceed as indicated in the instructions to Exercises 1–3.

Locrian mode – No. 3 [*H-W-W*] / No. 4 [*W-W-W*]

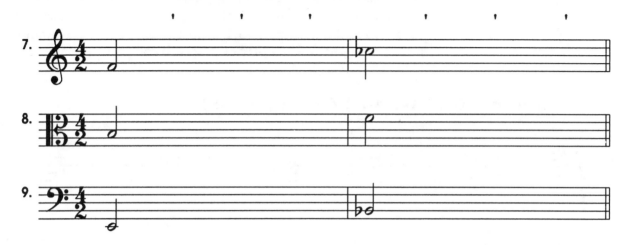

Instructions: Keeping in mind that modal tetrachord patterns remain the same whether they are ascending or descending, supply the missing pitches for the descending modes given in Exercises 10–12. Place each missing note under the spacing marker provided for good manuscript.

F Mixolydian

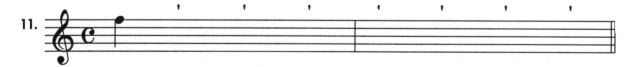

F Dorian

F Aeolian

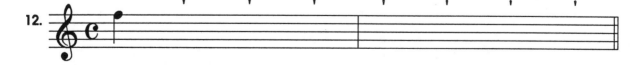

DRILL STUDY #4

Instructions: In Exercises 1–9, correct each poorly written measure in the blank measured spaces provided immediately below. The solution to the following exercises in simple-duple, simple-triple, and simple-quadruple time signatures will involve the knowledge and understanding of the principles of equal division, proper grouping, consolidation, as well as the application of beaming techniques.

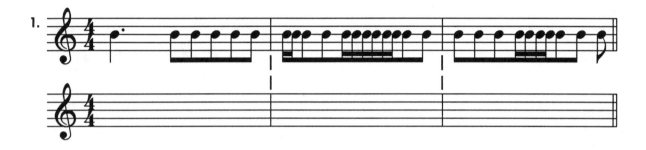

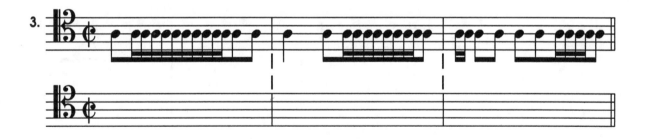

5.

6.

7.

8.

9.

ASSIGNMENT FOR CHAPTER 4

NAME _____ SCORE _____ GRADE _____

DATE DUE _____ SECTION _____ INSTRUCTOR _____

1. *Instructions:* Supply the missing pitches to the ascending and descending modes given in Parts (a)–(g). Be sure to alternate lines and spaces and to place each missing note directly under the spacing marker provided. When completed, play, hear, and identify each successive tetrachord combination of each modal scale.

2. *Instructions:* In Parts (a)–(e), correct each poorly written measure and place the corrected version in the blank measured spaces immediately below. Apply the principles of *equal division*, *proper grouping*, and *consolidation*. In addition use *ties* when the occasion demands it, and be sure to apply all of the *beaming* techniques learned in this chapter.

PERFORMANCE ASSIGNMENT FOR CHAPTER 4

Instructions: The following graded exercises (1–3) are meant to be used as an additional or optional assignment. They are challenging and performance-oriented exercises designed to monitor progress, understanding, and comprehension of the various rhythmical materials presented thus far. See the list, *Performance Terms and Expression Names* on pages 257–60.

Suggested Mode of Practice

The various parts of these exercises are meant to be sung, although they may be performed on various instruments by adjusting octave ranges and/or clefs. The preference for singing over other forms of study, such as handclapping or finger tapping, is to provide for a better understanding of "held" or long-duration note values. Start out by setting your metronome to the suggested tempo marking, and give yourself two complete measures of preparation before attempting to sing each part. If mistakes are made, it is better to continue on to the very end before solving the problems. Once you have experienced the entire part, it is then wise to go back to those troubled areas for further study and corrections. Make every effort to maintain the continuity of the beat. After completing each part to your satisfaction, observe the repeat symbol

:‖

placed at the end of each exercise; repeat as often as necessary to ensure complete understanding and excellence of performance.

1. Level I

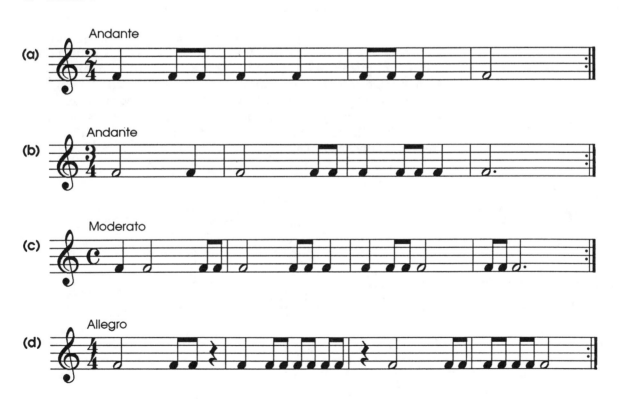

2. Level II

(a)

(b)

3. Level III

(a)

(b)

4. Duet or Classroom Drill

Suggested Mode of Practice

This exercise is meant to be sung as a duet for two students or as a classroom drill for two groups of performers. Each part is written on a different pitch level to help distinguish one part from another. Follow the directions given for levels I, II, and III, and attempt to listen simultaneously to all parts while performing the exercise. It is important that every effort be made to experience as many subtleties as possible. Participating in an ensemble performance can be extremely gratifying and enjoyable.

CHAPTER

5

MAJOR
SCALES
and
RHYTHM

Section

1

Pitch Considerations

DIATONIC MAJOR SCALES

In Chapter 4, the *Ionian mode* was represented as a scale that is placed within the architectural limits of one octave and that contains a certain pattern or mixture of half steps and whole steps. This pattern of the Ionian mode is common to all **diatonic major scales** and is the basis upon which all key signatures are derived. The word "**diatonic**," in this context, indicates a scale containing a mixture of half steps and whole steps and that is further designated as either a major or minor scale, as opposed to a chromatic scale. The Ionian mode constructed on c prime (c') is identical in sound and structure to that of the "C Major scale."

Example 51
The Ionian mode and the C major scale.

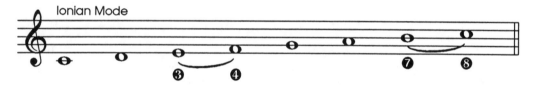

THE MAJOR TETRACHORD

The placement of half steps between the third and fourth and between the seventh and eighth degrees provides still another clue to the construction of major scales—the *major tetrachord*. This mixture of half steps and whole steps is the same tetrachord pattern previously introduced in Chapter 4 as Tetrachord No. 1. It may now also be referred to as the **major tetrachord**. The successive placement of two of these tetrachords—one after another and within the architectural limits of one octave—will yield each and every major scale possible within the tonal system. In addition, the writing of major scales in this manner will show the derivation of each individual **key signature** (the sharps or flats appearing at the beginning of a staff, indicating the scale and key of a composition).

In Example 52, carefully examine the complete series for these pertinent points of understanding:

- the construction of each major tetrachord;
- the sequential and systematic use of major tetrachords;
- the relative position of the major tetrachords within each scale;
- the separation of a whole step between major tetrachords;
- the systematic placement of each *sharp* and *flat*; and
- the resulting *key signature*.

Example 52
The application of the major tetrachord.

(a) E♭ major

(b) B♭ major

(c) F major

(d) C major

(e) G major

(f) D major

If one continues the process of making the second tetrachord of the preceding scale the first tetrachord of a new scale, *all fifteen major keys* with their *key signatures* will evolve. The fifteen major-key areas are distributed in the following manner: seven flat keys; seven sharp keys; plus the key of "C" with no sharps or flats.

As a point of information, the key signatures of B and C♭ major, F♯ and G♭ major, C♯ and D♭ major are enharmonically equivalent; although sounding the same, they are written differently. Hence, although fifteen individual major keys are practical and are employed regularly by the musician, only twelve possible pitches are within the compass of one octave. (Three major keys must remain enharmonically the same.)

KEY SIGNATURES

Through careful examination, it has been found that a major key is derived from the all-important Ionian pattern of whole steps and half steps and that a key signature is always placed at the beginning of each staff, directly after the clef sign. The placement of the key signature provides the performer with important information regarding certain pitches of the key. Unlike individually placed accidentals within the body of a composition, those of the key signature affect all of the pitches to which they refer in all octaves and measures, unless otherwise altered and notated. Understanding this very important concept is critical to the successful performance of a given composition.

In Tables 7 and 8 on pages 94 and 95, carefully examine each clef sign and its corresponding set of key signatures. In addition, be sure to notice that the placement order of sharps in the tenor clef is different than that of the treble, alto, and bass clefs.

NOTATING MAJOR SCALES

The act of actually notating major scales deserves major attention. The following pertinent points and examples should clear up any misunderstandings that might arise in their construction.

1. Begin by placing the desired clef and octave **keynotes** (starting pitches) in position on the staff provided.

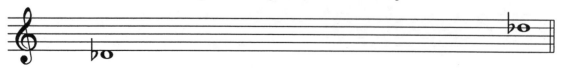

2. Next, place a pitch on each *alternating line and space*. Be careful to observe the principles of good manuscript.

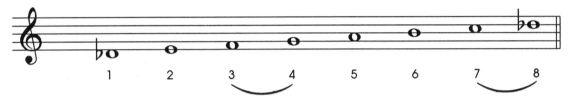

3. Place a scale-step number directly underneath each pitch and indicate each half step with a curved line. The half-step pattern is found between scale steps 3 and 4 and between 7 and 8.

4. Superimpose two successive major tetrachords [Tetrachord No. 1] one after another on the scale and begin to derive each scale degree and its ensuing *key signature*.

5. Place the derived group of accidentals (key signature) to the right of the clef and before the first scale degree in the following order:

Bb, Eb, Ab, Db, and Gb

The flats that are placed on the scale and in parenthesis are used here to demonstrate how the process of notating a scale evolves; however, in practice, accidentals placed in parenthesis serve merely as *reminders* to the performer and are not necessary or required for the writing of good manuscript. They are used at the discretion of the composer, orchestrator, or copyist as an editing device.

6. The concluding result and proper manuscript for the key signature and major scale of Db major follows:

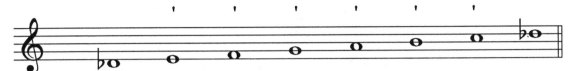

Table 7 ▪ *Major Key Signatures in Treble and Bass Clefs*

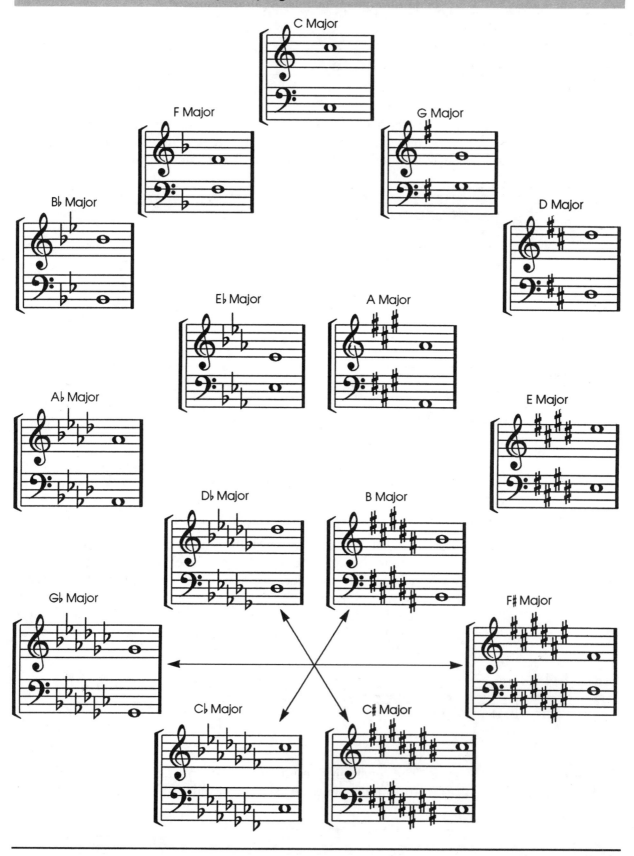

Table 8 ▪ *Major Key Signatures in Alto and Tenor Clefs*

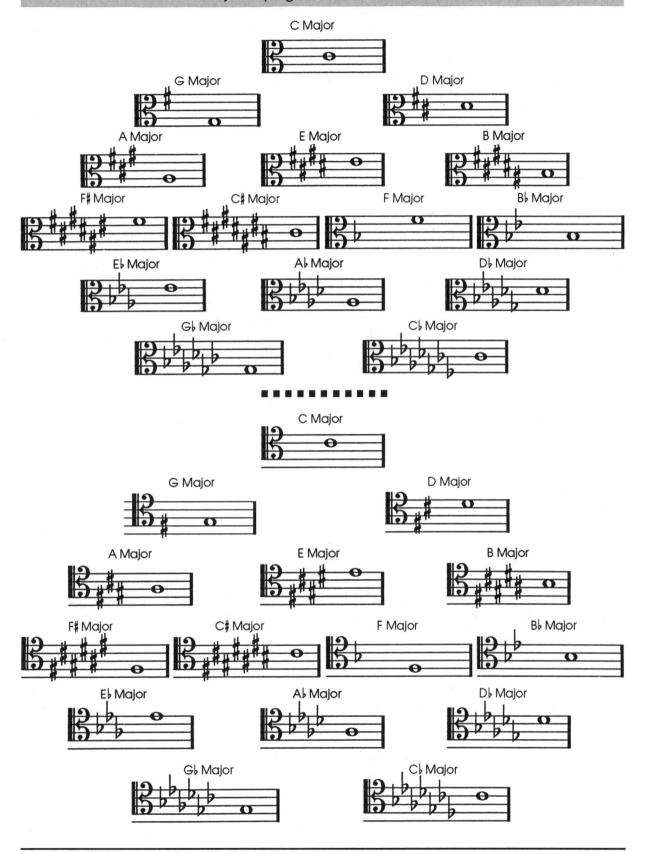

The specific placement of accidentals within a key signature is chiefly determined by visual logic and not some esoteric, theoretical concept. Also, the scale order of sharps or flats in a major scale is *not* related to the placement of a key signature. The overriding consideration in placement is ease in reading. The student should memorize the traditional placement of sharps or flats for each key signature and, in addition, memorize them in the soprano, alto, tenor, and bass clefs.

THE USE OF ACCIDENTALS

Finally, it is important that some comment be made concerning a pertinent area of performance: the use of accidentals. In the study of key signatures, we have seen that a group of accidentals can affect those tones to which they refer in all octaves and measures. But what about accidentals that are placed in the body of the composition and are not part of the key signature? What is presently the practice and what has it been traditionally?

Any accidental used to affect or alter a pitch is for that specific pitch and not for its upper or lower octaves. The alteration remains in force for the duration of one measure only, unless tied over a bar line to a note in the next measure. If and when this takes place, the altered pitch remains in effect for the duration of the tie and not for the entire measure.

Perhaps the best way to explain these procedures is to present a musical example with all of the conditions present.

Example 53
The use of accidentals

❶ The accidental is introduced, but

❷ and ❸ it does not affect other octaves—sharps in parenthesis are simply reminders to performers.

❹ The accidental (alteration) is still in effect.

❺ The tie extends the duration of the accidental for the length of the tie only, and

❻ the last two beats of measure two revert to the key signature.

Section

2

The Notation of Rhythm

OVER THE SPLIT

In Chapter 4, the notating of rhythmic groupings in quadruple time was governed primarily by the concept of *equal division* and the imaginary placement of the so-called *split*. Certain rules governing the content of either side of the split were introduced and developed. The final phase of understanding involves the *two exceptions* to equal division, and the imaginary split placed between the upbeat of two and the downbeat of three in a measure of quadruple time, referred to as "**over the split**." Although beaming over the split is not recommended, the duration of time or the choice of note value selected for placement is another matter. Duration or the note of choice in this case makes reference to the beat or the unit of measure. The beat is symbolized by the lower number of the time signature—the *denominator*. If the time signature is $\frac{4}{4}$ time, the unit of measure is a quarter note. Hence, the rule that follows states that *no more than a single unit* may be placed "over the split" in quadruple time in accordance with the *denominator* of the time signature. A closer look at this concept can best be described and shown in the ensuing discussion of *syncopation*.

EXCEPTIONS TO EQUAL DIVISION

Syncopation—the act of giving prominence to a normally unaccented beat or fraction of a beat by lengthening the duration of its sound—serves as Category I of *exceptions* to the principle of equal division. It also serves to describe the word "duration" and the phrase "unit of measure" as they involve the imaginary *split* in quadruple time. Although definitions of *syncopation* are varied and sometimes broader, the definition given here is more concise and definitive in the understanding of rhythmic notation. Study the two measures presented in Example 54. The top version exemplifies syncopation without the use of the "over the split" exception. Although the bottom version is scored differently, the sound of the two measures is exactly the same; moreover, the bottom version utilizes the "over the split" exception, which, in this case, is the durational limit of one quarter note. Both measures in the example are rhythmically correct and, indeed, are used extensively in written music.

Example 54

Syncopation.

(a) Consistent with equal division:

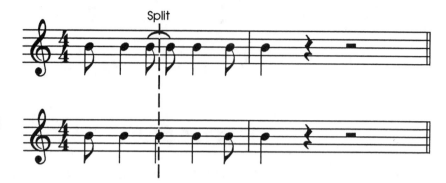

(b) The exception to equal division:

A good visual understanding of syncopation is important to the performance of this unique rhythmic sound in music. The ability to utilize one's visual impression through imagery and memorization will help establish an understanding of this rhythmic sound. The following exercise is presented in the form of three drills that are intended to yield a strong foundation for performance. Part (a) is presented in quadruple time and is written as an *exception* to equal division; it is the same as Part (a) of Exercise 54. Part (b) is presented in triple time and does *not* utilize equal division; however, it is consolidated and is consistent with certain principles of equal division. Part (c) is presented in *duple* time, which can be looked upon as half of quadruple time. Although equal division is *not* utilized in duple meter, the principles are the same as they would be for either side of the imaginary split in quadruple time. When notating triple or duple time, the most important principles to remember are proper grouping and consolidation.

In Drills (a)–(c) of Example 55, *repetition* is very important. Perform each drill several times, individually. Then perform the drills one after another as a single exercise. Again, repeating the entire study several times is very important. Commit it to memory and make it a daily routine. Individually numbered beats and arrows are provided to ensure a better understanding of the stress of the accented and normally unaccented beats. In each drill give yourself a four-beat preparation. The thin-and-thick double line preceded by two dots, :‖, at the end of each study is the symbol for indicating a repeated expression in music.

Example 55

Three syncopation drills.

(a)

(b)

Category II of exceptions to the principle of equal division involves a set of four simple measures. These measures are precise and are clearly notated in order to demonstrate the complete absence of the split. In addition, the use of variation is introduced; this becomes an integral part of the overall concept. In each measure it is important to observe where each exception takes place and, also, to observe how the use of variation is integrated within the measure. Every effort should be made to memorize these four simple measures and to remember how the variations are applied.

Example 56
Exceptions to equal division.

Variations of exceptions to equal division.

In measure one (1), variations of a whole note as a note value do not exist. The rectangular screens placed around the note values in measures two (2), three (3), and four (4) represent the rhythmic exceptions and are not part of the variations. Only six variations are given, but countless others exist. If asked, could you provide several others?

MANUSCRIPT TIPS

Bar-line structures: Different types of bar-line structures in music manuscript play an important role in delineating measures, sections, and ends of compositions. Often, the very essence of a composition, in terms of its architectural structure or form, is outlined by the use of particular bar lines. More specifically, bar lines contribute to the overall musical coherence of a composition and thereby provide the performer with valuable information. Three bar-line structures are presented for study:

A single bar line indicates the beginning or ending of a measure.

Two bar lines (double bar) placed closely together designate the end of a section within a composition.

Two bar lines (also called a double bar) placed closely together, with one thin line and the other somewhat thicker, designate the end of a composition.

Manuscript Practice

Use these manuscript pages for note taking and drill.

DRILL STUDY #1

Instructions: Exercises 1–7 are designed to teach the writing of *major scales* and the derivation of their *key signatures*. In each exercise, the top staff is for incorporating the five-step process as presented on pages 92–93. The bottom staff is to serve as the finished product as seen on page 93, step 6. Follow each direction carefully and include clef signs, keynotes, half-step indicators, numbers, brackets, accidentals, tetrachord patterns, parentheses, and key signatures. Place the notes under the spacing markers provided. Refer regularly to pages 94–95 for correct key-signature placement.

1. E major [Keynote e' Ascending—Treble Clef]

(a)

(b)

2. A♭ major [Keynote a♭' Ascending—Treble Clef]

(a)

(b)

3. D major [Keynote d' Ascending—Treble Clef]

(a)

(b)

4. B♭ major [Keynote B♭ Ascending—Bass Clef]

(a)

(b)

5. F♯ major [Keynote F♯ Ascending—Bass Clef]

(a)

(b)

6. D♭ major [Keynote d♭ Ascending—Alto Clef]

(a)

(b)

7. A major [Keynote A Ascending—Tenor Clef]

(a)

(b)

DRILL STUDY #2

Instructions: Exercises 1–4 are meant to provide a necessary drill for the exact order and placement of each sharp or flat within a key signature. Study each clef example presented and supply, under the spacing markers provided, the missing sharps or flats as well as the necessary clef sign for each given key signature.

1. The placement of *sharps* in treble clef.

C♯ major

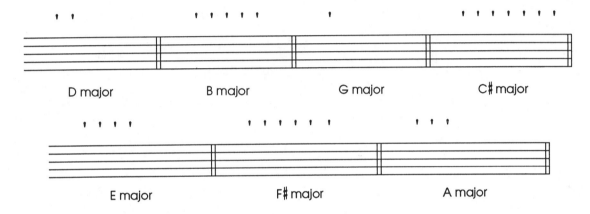

D major   B major   G major   C♯ major

E major   F♯ major   A major

2. The placement of *flats* in treble clef.

C♭ major

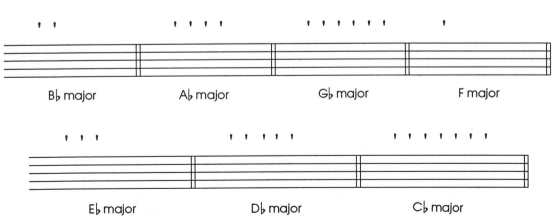

B♭ major   A♭ major   G♭ major   F major

E♭ major   D♭ major   C♭ major

3. The placement of *sharps* in bass clef.

C♯ major

D major   E major   G major   A major

F♯ major   B major   C♯ major

4. The placement of *flats* in bass clef.

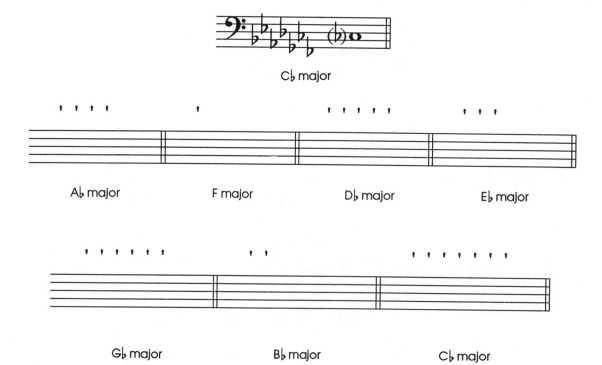

C♭ major

A♭ major   F major   D♭ major   E♭ major

G♭ major   B♭ major   C♭ major

DRILL STUDY #3

Instructions: Exercises 1–4 are meant to provide a necessary drill for the exact order and placement of each sharp or flat within a key signature. Study each clef example presented and supply, under the spacing markers provided, the missing sharps or flats as well as the necessary clef sign for each given key signature.

1. The placement of *sharps* in the alto clef.

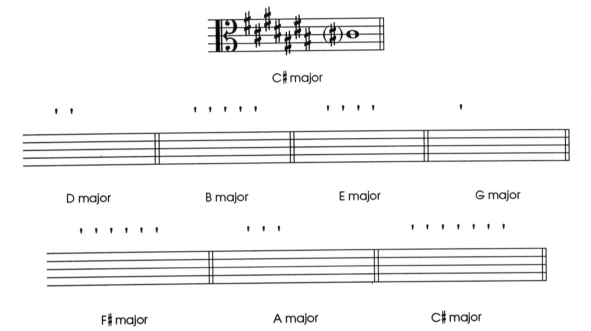

C♯ major

D major   B major   E major   G major

F♯ major   A major   C♯ major

2. The placement of *flats* in the alto clef.

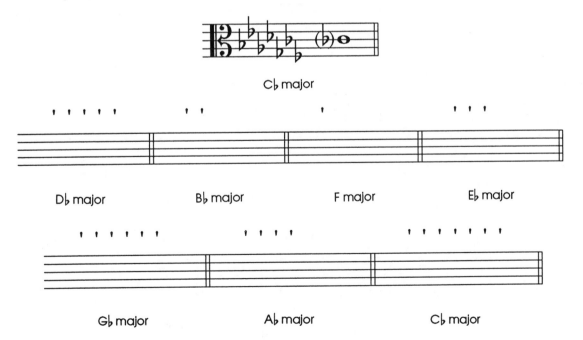

C♭ major

D♭ major   B♭ major   F major   E♭ major

G♭ major   A♭ major   C♭ major

3. The placement of *sharps* in tenor clef.

C♯ major

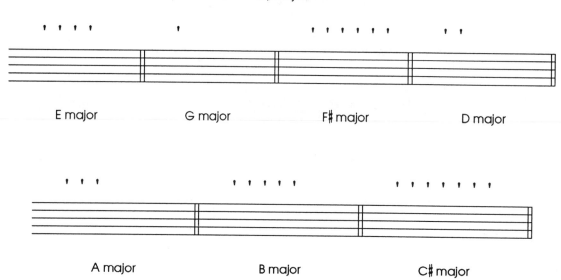

E major   G major   F♯ major   D major

A major   B major   C♯ major

4. The placement of *flats* in tenor clef.

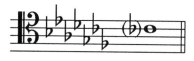

C♭ major

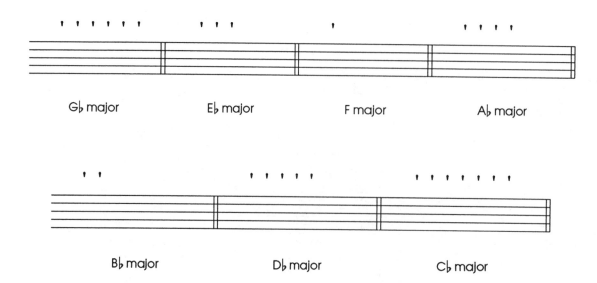

G♭ major   E♭ major   F major   A♭ major

B♭ major   D♭ major   C♭ major

DRILL STUDY #4

1. *Instructions:* In Parts (a)–(d), correct each poorly written measure and place the corrected version in the blank measured spaces immediately below. Apply the principles of *equal division, proper grouping,* and *consolidation.* In addition, use ties when the occasion demands them and be sure to apply all of the beaming techniques learned as well as the new concepts relating to *over the split.* More than one solution may be possible in some measures.

2. *Instructions:* In the following exercises correct each poorly written measure as outlined in the instructions to Exercise 1; however, consolidation and grouping problems will be mixed in with exception Categories I and II. In some exercises two solutions exist. You may choose either the syncopation or the equal-division solution. More than one solution may be possible in some measures.

ASSIGNMENT FOR CHAPTER 5

NAME _____ SCORE _____ GRADE _____

DATE DUE _____ SECTION _____ INSTRUCTOR _____

1. *Instructions:* On the staffs provided in Parts (a)–(e), supply the proper clef, key signature, and ascending-scale notation for each given keynote. Good manuscript is of paramount importance.

(a) E♭ major (Treble Clef)

(b) B major (Alto Clef)

(c) A major (Bass Clef)

(d) F♯ major (Treble Clef)

(e) D♭ major (Tenor Clef)

2. *Instructions:* Supply the designated clef and key signature in each blank measure provided in Parts (a)–(d). Since the practice of good manuscript is of paramount importance, every effort should be made to draw each key signature accurately.

(a) Treble Clef

| D major | A♭ major | E major | G♭ major | A major |

(b) Alto Clef

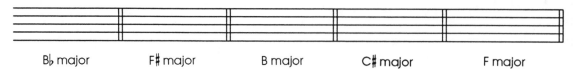

| B♭ major | F♯ major | B major | C♯ major | F major |

(c) Tenor Clef

| G♭ major | D major | E major | C♭ major | G major |

(d) Bass Clef

| E♭ major | C major | A♭ major | D♭ major | A major |

3. *Instructions:* In Parts (a) and (b), correct each poorly written measure and place the corrected version in the blank measured space immediately below. Apply all of the principles of correct rhythmic notation and be sure to include the two categories of exceptions to equal division. More than one solution may be possible in some measures.

4. *Instructions:* Fill in the following blanks in accordance with the use of accidentals.

(a) If a tie is used over a bar line involving an accidental, the alteration remains in force for the duration of the _____ , and not for the entire measure.

(b) An accidental used to affect or alter a pitch is for that specific pitch, and not its_____ or _____ octaves.

PERFORMANCE ASSIGNMENT FOR CHAPTER 5

Instructions: The following graded exercises are meant to be used as an additional or optional assignment. Written in the same manner as the previous performance assignments, they are challenging and performance-oriented exercises designed to monitor progress, understanding, and comprehension of the various rhythmical materials presented thus far.

Suggested Mode of Practice

Again, as in the Performance Assignment for Chapter 4, the various parts of these exercises are meant to be sung, although they may be performed on various instruments by adjusting octave ranges and/or clefs. The preference for singing over other forms of study, such as handclapping or finger tapping, is to provide for a better understanding of "held" or long-duration note values. Again, start out by setting your metronome to the suggested tempo marking, and give yourself two complete measures of preparation before attempting to sing each part. If mistakes are made, it is better to continue on to the very end before solving the problems. Once you have experienced the entire part, it is then wise to go back to those troubled areas for further study and corrections. Make every effort to maintain the continuity of the beat. When all the parts have been completed to your satisfaction, repeat them several times to ensure complete understanding and excellence of performance.

1. Level I

2. Level II

(a)

(b)

(c)

(d)

3. Level III

(a)

(b)

(c)

(d)

CHAPTER

6

MINOR
SCALES
and
RHYTHM

Section

1

Pitch Considerations

DIATONIC MINOR SCALES

In Chapter 5, the pattern of the *Ionian mode* was shown as the basis for *major scales* and for the subsequent organization of key signatures. By a similar method, the *Aeolian mode* may act as the basis for *diatonic minor scales* and their key signatures. The mixture or pattern of whole steps and half steps found in the Aeolian mode is identical in sound and construction with that of the Aeolian form of the A minor scale.

Example 57
The Aeolian mode and the Aeolian form of the minor scale.

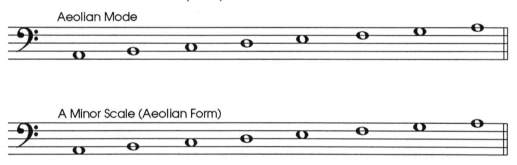

THE AEOLIAN, HARMONIC, AND MELODIC FORMS

There are three forms of the minor—the *Aeolian form*, shown in Example 57, the *harmonic form*, and the *melodic form*. The **Aeolian form**, sometimes referred to as the **natural** or **pure form**, was thought by theorists and composers to be inconclusive and, therefore, inappropriate for melodic and harmonic stability and finality. From this reasoning and through a composing device referred to as *musica ficta* (fictitious music), certain adjustments in the upper tetrachord of the scale were imposed upon the Aeolian to produce more conclusively sounding scale forms.

The lack of finality or conclusiveness in the Aeolian was overcome by raising the seventh degree of the scale by one half step. This created a scale with a more desirable feeling of finality and was, henceforth, referred to as the **harmonic form** of the minor. The notion of raising the seventh degree to achieve a more final or more tonal feeling was borrowed from the pattern of the major scale.

Example 58

The A major scale and harmonic form of the minor.

A Major Scale

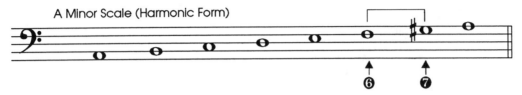

A Minor Scale (Harmonic Form)

The interval created between the sixth and seventh degrees, however, was considered to be nonvocal and inconsistent with the normal character of European music and this, in turn, gave rise to the third form of the minor, the *melodic* form. With the addition of more *musica ficta*, the **melodic form** was developed, as shown in Example 59. The adjustments overcame all objections, but resulted in the formation of two different patterns—the **ascending form**, in which the sixth and seventh degrees were both raised one half step, and the **descending form**, in which the sixth and seventh degrees were both lowered or restored to their original Aeolian form.

Example 59

Melodic form of the minor.

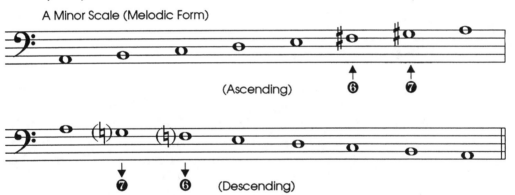

A Minor Scale (Melodic Form)

(Ascending)

(Descending)

Although the three scale forms of the minor are individually unique, they involve, perhaps, the most prominent feature of the entire minor-scale concept; *all three forms share the same tonic minor tetrachord.* The **tonic tetrachord**, which is found in both major and minor scales, is located on the keynote or starting pitch of the scale. Additionally, the identification of a particular form of the minor scale depends entirely on the pattern of the second tetrachord, whose starting pitch is located on the fifth degree of the scale. This tetrachord is referred to as the **dominant tetrachord** and its pitch contents vary with each form of the minor scale. In Example 60, the minor-scale forms are shown and are labeled accordingly.

Example 60

Forms of the A minor scale.

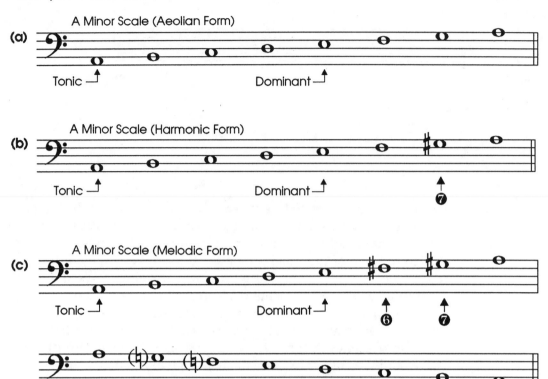

THE PARALLEL SYSTEM

A minor scale can function in two ways within the diatonic scale system. It can be considered *parallel* or *relative*, depending upon its relationship to a given major tonality. In order that a minor scale be referred to as **parallel**, it must *share* each of the identical tonal degrees of the major tonality to which it is compared. Tonal pitches that help to form the key are found on the *first* (**tonic**), the *fourth* (**subdominant**), and the *fifth* (**dominant**) degrees of each diatonic major and minor scale. The *second* (**supertonic**), *third* (**mediant**), *sixth* (**submediant**), and *seventh* (**leading tone**) degrees are changeable and, therefore, are referred to as the **modal pitches of the scale**.

Example 61

Tonal and modal degrees of the major scale.

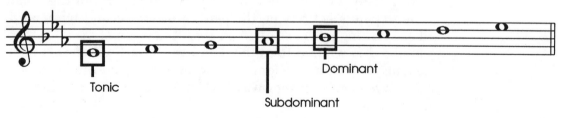

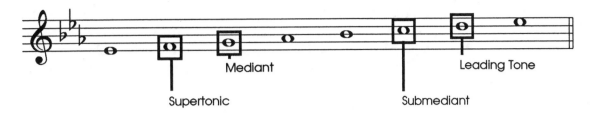

Supertonic Mediant Submediant Leading Tone

Although tonal degrees are shared by both parallel major and minor scales of their respective tonalities, they do *not* share the same key signature. Thus, F major, with a key signature of one flat, has a parallel minor tonality of F minor which, in turn, has a key signature of four flats.

Imagine the composing potential provided by this interchangeability of the major and the parallel minor tonalities! This capability illustrates a device that has long been used by the great composers of the world.

Example 62

The parallel major and minor scale forms.

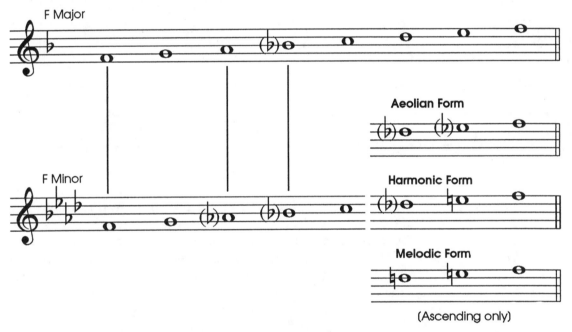

F Major

F Minor

Aeolian Form

Harmonic Form

Melodic Form

(Ascending only)

THE RELATIVE SYSTEM

Previously, it was stated that a minor scale can function in two ways within the diatonic scale system. It can share the tonal degrees of the major scale to which it is compared and, therefore, be considered *parallel*, or it can be shown in relationship with that of a major tonality and be considered *relative*.

In order that a minor scale be referred to as **relative**, its keynote must be located on the *sixth* or *submediant degree* of the related major scale. Additionally, it must share the identical key signature of its related major when an Aeolian mode is formed on its keynote. In Example 63, study each label presented and the relationship between scales; two samples of the *relative* system are presented for study.

Example 63

The relative system.

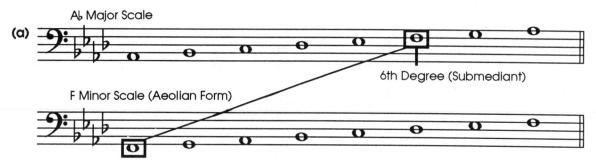

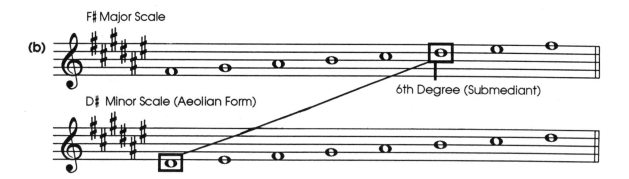

The relationship of the minor scale with its *relative*-major key signature creates a situation in which fifteen key signatures may now be interpreted as being both major and minor. The method for determining the actual key signature of a composition is governed by musical context and other more profound considerations. However, the fact still remains that any key signature may now be interpreted as a major or minor tonality. This system of sharing or dual function is found throughout the entire diatonic key-signature system. In Table 9, fifteen major/minor key signatures are presented for study and memorization.

To understand the relative-minor system fully, two samples are presented for further study in Example 64 on page 122. Sample (a) presents the relationship of the major key to its relative minor and its three different forms. The presentation of the minor scale with its three forms and its relationship to its relative-major scale is shown in Sample (b). Note carefully in both samples the sharing of key signatures, the relationship and location of keynotes or tonics of each scale, and the use of *musica ficta*, as it relates to the *harmonic* and *melodic* forms of the minor scales.

Table 9 ▪ *Major/Minor Signatures in Treble and Bass Clefs*

Example 64

The relative system.

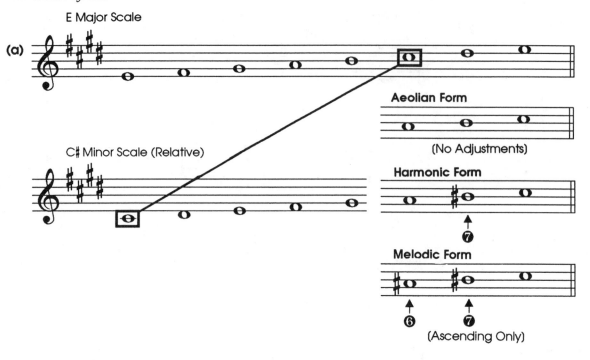

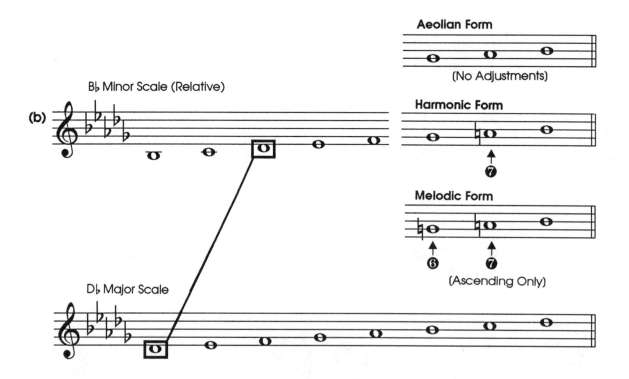

A REVIEW OF MINOR SCALES

Here is a step-by-step summation that reviews minor scales and their various forms. All minor scales are either *parallel* or *relative*, depending upon their relationship to a given major tonality.

The following pertinent points apply to *parallel minor scales*:

1. All parallel minor scales share the same tonal degrees of the parallel major scale to which they are compared.
2. Although both scales—the major and the parallel minor—share the same tonic keynotes, they do *not* share the same key signature.
3. All parallel minor scales utilize the three forms of the minor: the *Aeolian*, the *harmonic*, and the *melodic*.

The following important points apply to *relative minor scales*:

1. All relative minor scales share the same key signatures as their related major scales.
2. All keynotes or starting notes of each relative minor scale begin on the sixth degree of their related major scales.
3. All relative minor scales utilize the three forms of the minor: the *Aeolian*, the *harmonic*, and the *melodic*.

The various forms of minor scales are constructed as follows:

1. The *Aeolian* or *natural form* of the minor is identical in sound and construction with that of the *Aeolian mode*, and it does *not* require any adjustment to its scale.
2. The *harmonic* form of the Aeolian mode or natural minor scale utilizes a raised seventh degree in its scale, ascending as well as descending. The adjustments or accidentals are applied to the scale or the body of the composition whenever needed; traditionally, they are *never* applied to the key signature.
3. The *melodic* form of the Aeolian mode or natural minor scale utilizes a raised sixth and seventh degree in its scale ascending and a lowered sixth and seventh descending. The accidentals are applied to the scale or the body of the composition whenever needed; traditionally, they are *never* applied to the key signature.

THE DOMINANT HARMONIC MINOR TETRACHORD

In order to create the three separate forms of the minor, it will be necessary to introduce an additional tetrachord. For the purpose of identification, this tetrachord will be called the **Dominant Harmonic Minor Tetrachord No. 5**; it is presented in Example 65. Its construction is characterized by the one-and-one-half-step interval found between the second and third pitches. In addition, this tetrachord is placed on the dominant degree (V) of the harmonic minor and becomes the 5th, 6th, 7th, and 8th degrees of the scale. See Table 5, The Four Modal Tetrachord Patterns, on page 67, for a quick review of the previously introduced tetrachords.

Example 65
Tetrachord No. 5.

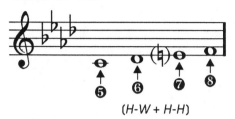

(H-W + H-H)

The three forms of the minor are formed in the following manner:

Aeolian Form = Tetrachord No. 2 followed by Tetrachord No. 3
For example: FGA♭B♭ CD♭E♭F

Harmonic Form = Tetrachord No. 2 followed by Tetrachord No. 5
For example: FGA♭B♭ CD♭E♮F

Melodic Form = Tetrachord No. 2 followed by Tetrachord No. 1
For example: FGA♭B♭ CD♮E♮F

Also, **descending form** is the same as Aeolian form but with Tetrachord No. 3 followed by Tetrachord No. 2.

A METHOD FOR DETERMINING MINOR KEY SIGNATURES

In order to determine the key signature of a minor key quickly, simply count up one-and-one-half steps from the keynote and make a three-letter name change to ensure the proper interval distance. When both of these requirements have been met, the name of the relative-major key signature will be provided; hence, the key signature of C minor is the same as that of E♭ major—each has three flats.

The method just described requires that a three-letter name change be effected from the minor keynote of c, which results in the letter name e. Additionally, the distance of one-and-one-half steps should be calculated from c to e♭. It should be indicated, however, that although d♯ constitutes a distance of one-and-one-half steps upward, it could not be the proper response because the letter name only involves a two-letter name change from c. The correct response can only be E♭.

Section

2

The Notation of Rhythm

THE USE OF REST VALUES

In earlier chapters and in various drill studies, note values and their equivalent rest values in simple time have been presented for study; however, specific information as to the use of rest values was not complete. At this point, further information on this topic is needed.

Symbols that consist of measured silence in modern traditional practice include the *double whole rest*, the *whole rest*, the *half rest*, the *quarter rest*, the *eighth rest*, the *sixteenth rest*, the *thirty-second rest*, the *sixty-fourth rest*, and the *one-hundred twenty-eighth rest*. Moreover, these symbols of exact duration are placed precisely within the normal division of the measure unit as well as within the normal division of the measure. In simpler terms, as a rule, a rest symbol occupies the same position in a given measure that an equivalent note value would fill. (There is one important exception to this rule, and it will be presented in *Manuscript Tips*, on page 129.)

Example 66
The placement of note values and rest values.

THE WHOLE REST

Although the **whole rest** contains the value of a whole note, it has become the universal symbol for any completely silent measure, regardless of the time signature. It serves as the whole-measure rest for time signatures from $\frac{8}{2}$ to $\frac{3}{16}$ time; however, as shown in the last measure of Example 67, time signatures of smaller duration employ the actual-value rest symbol for a completely rested measure.

Example 67
Rest symbols for completely rested measures.

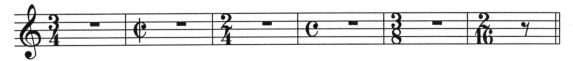

The whole rest must *not* be used to indicate a fractional part of a measure, except in $\frac{4}{2}$ time. The problem presents itself when half the measure is rested. The recommended solution involves the use of the whole rest as a half-measure rest instead of two individual half rests. The following example is one of very few exceptions to the use of the universal whole-rest symbol.

Example 68
An exceptional use of the universal whole-rest symbol.

(Recommended)   (Unacceptable)

If two consecutive beats of a triple time signature, such as $\frac{3}{2}$ time, are rested, individual half rests must be used to eliminate the fractional appearance of a whole rest. In $\frac{6}{4}$ time, when the last four consecutive beats are rested, the recommended solution is a quarter rest followed by a dotted half rest. (The topic of proper grouping in compound meters will be discussed in detail in the next chapter.)

Example 69
Solutions to fractional presentations of a whole rest.

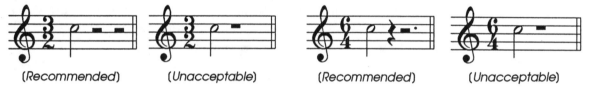

(Recommended)   (Unacceptable)   (Recommended)   (Unacceptable)

THE HALF REST

The **half rest** is so-called because it is one-half the value of a whole rest. It is drawn as an oblong mark of about the same length as the whole rest. It is located on top of the third line of the staff in time signatures in which it can express the rested half of an equally divided time signature. Because of this rule, the half rest is *never* found in triple time. Study the recommended solutions and the comparative representations in Example 70 for a more concise understanding of the *nonuse* of half rests in triple time.

Example 70
The nonuse of half rests in triple time.

(Recommended)   (Unacceptable)

In duple (cut-time) and quadruple-time signatures in which the measure can be equally divided, the placement of the half rest is critical. Its placement must represent two combined quarter rests on either side of the split, or, to put it another way, on either side of the two equally divided parts of the measure. Unlike its note-value counterpart, the half rest can *never* occupy an overlapping position (over the split) within the measure. In Example 71, study the important relationship of the equally divided parts of the measure and the recommended use of the quarter rests in place of the half rest.

Example 71
The nonuse of the half rest in an overlapping position within a measure.

THE QUARTER REST

As was stated earlier, the **quarter rest** (one-quarter the value of a whole rest) is perhaps the most difficult rest symbol to draw; in music manuscript, it is the one symbol that is represented with a certain degree of artistic freedom. As with any proper rest symbol, the placement of the quarter rest is governed, largely, by the unit of measure (the beat) and the normal division of the time signature.

In the first measure of Example 72, the combination of the upbeat of two and the downbeat of three is shown as the syncopation exception to equal division. It is the quarter note that is recommended. In the second measure, individual eighth rests are provided according to the equal-division principle and are recommended because they do not upset or obscure the normal division of the measure. The quarter rest, however, placed in measure three is unacceptable because it obscures the normal division of the measure, even though when used as a *note value*, it is acceptable.

Example 72
Equal divisions and syncopation exceptions with note values and rest values.

NOTE-VALUE AND REST-VALUE ERRORS

This section is provided to help eliminate various common errors often seen in the writing of note values and rest values. What is commonly understood about note values is often misunderstood about rest values, and vice versa. Example 73 will present solutions to these commonly found errors of notation in music manuscript.

Perhaps the errors most often found in music manuscript involve the tied beamed eighth-note duplet, the tied quarter-note grouping, and the tied half-note grouping, as well as their rest-value counterparts. The tied beamed eighth-note duplet is completely erroneous and should *never* be written. With the exception of the tied beamed eighth-note duplet, each of the other groupings are most often erroneous. At this point in our studies, it might be wise to reiterate that "old saw" that rests can *never* be literally tied. Study the following commonly found errors and suggested solutions presented as partial measure groupings and as completed measures of music.

Example 73

Errors in note values and rest values.

(a)

Never write a tied, beamed eighth duplet. Always write the equivalent quarter note.

Do not tie rests. Always write the equivalent quarter-rest symbol.

(b)

Do not use a tied quarter-note grouping instead of a half note on each side of the split in quadruple time.

Do not use a quarter-rest grouping instead of a half rest on each side of the split in quadruple time.

A tied quarter-note grouping is quite acceptable, and is recommended in this instance. One could not utilize the half note in its place.

(c)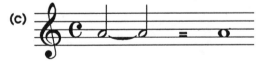

Do not tie a half-note grouping within the measure; use a whole note instead.

Do not tie rests in any meter. In quadruple time use the universal whole rest.

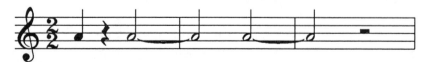

A tied half-note grouping over the bar line is recommended. One could not use a whole note in its place. Half-note rest symbols on each side of the bar line would be acceptable and would be recommended. However, they should not be tied in any case.

DOTTING RESTS IN SIMPLE TIME

The dotting of rests in simple time is governed primarily by the concept of normal division involving the beat as well as the measure of a given time signature. In simple time, rest values are almost *never* dotted. The one exception to this rule is that in simple time, rest symbols are to be dotted only within the confines of an individual beat when it is partially rested. Study the following measures for a more graphic display of this very important concept.

Example 74
The nonuse of dotted rests in simple time and the exception.

(Recommended)   (Unacceptable)   (The exception)

MANUSCRIPT TIPS

It was previously stated that rest values—and specifically, the whole rest—occupy the same position in a measure as those of equivalent note values. All of what has been presented so far concerns the notation of melodic and rhythmic design for single-line music (music written for an individual voice or instrument). For music scored in parts, such as in harmony in which more than one part is written on a staff, one exception exists. It concerns the whole note and the whole rest. In the scoring of parts in harmony in which a whole note or its equivalent rest value is used in one part and rhythmic movement is presented in other parts, the whole note or its equivalent rest value is no longer placed in the center of the measure but, rather, is moved to the left and is aligned with the first beat of the measure. To understand this concept better, a harmony example involving four voices is presented in Example 75. The soprano and alto parts are written in the treble clef, while the tenor and bass parts are shown in the bass clef. Note the placement of the whole note and whole rest in the first measure.

Example 75
The placement of the whole note and whole rest in part writing.

Manuscript Practice

Use these manuscript pages for note taking and drill.

DRILL STUDY #1

Instructions: In Exercises 1–5, place the missing second and third pitches of the Dominant Harmonic Minor Tetrachord No. 5 within the tetrachord limits provided. Be sure to alternate lines and spaces and to space the missing pitches equally for good manuscript.

Tetrachord No. 5 – [*H-W + H-H*]

Instructions: In Exercises 6–13, write the ascending and/or descending forms of the minor scale. Be sure to alternate lines and spaces. Space each scale degree equally for good manuscript. Provide the *clef, key signature,* and the *exact form of the minor scale.* If any accidentals are needed, place them within the body of the scale.

6. Treble Clef, G Minor, Aeolian Form, Ascending Only

7. Bass Clef, F Minor, Harmonic Form, Ascending Only

8. Treble Clef, A♭ Minor, Harmonic Form, Descending Only

9. Bass Clef, B Minor, Melodic Form, (Ascending and Descending)

10. Alto Clef, F♯ Minor, Harmonic Form, Ascending Only

11. Treble Clef, C Minor, Melodic Form, (Ascending and Descending)

12. Tenor Clef, E Minor, Aeolian Form, Descending Only

13. Bass Clef, G♯ Minor, Melodic Form, (Ascending and Descending)

DRILL STUDY #2

Instructions: Exercises 1–15 are designed to facilitate a quick response in determining the keynote of the relative minor when given the name of the *major key*. In order to determine the keynote (starting note) of any relative minor scale, simply count up six degrees of any major scale. Use Exercise 1 as a model for subsequent exercises and fill in the blanks.

1. __B__ minor is the relative minor of __D__ major.

2. _____ minor is the relative minor of __G__ major.

3. _____ minor is the relative minor of __F♯__ major.

4. _____ minor is the relative minor of __A__ major.

5. _____ minor is the relative minor of __B♭__ major.

6. _____ minor is the relative minor of __C__ major.

7. _____ minor is the relative minor of __F__ major.

8. _____ minor is the relative minor of __D♭__ major.

9. _____ minor is the relative minor of __A♭__ major.

10. _____ minor is the relative minor of __G♭__ major.

11. _____ minor is the relative minor of __C♯__ major.

12. _____ minor is the relative minor of __E♭__ major.

13. _____ minor is the relative minor of __C♭__ major.

14. _____ minor is the relative minor of __B__ major.

15. _____ minor is the relative minor of __E__ major.

Instructions: Exercises 16–30 are designed to facilitate a quick response in determining the keynote of the relative major when given the name of the *minor key*. In order to determine the keynote of any relative major scale, simply count up one-and-one-half steps and make a three-letter change. Use Exercise 16 as a model for subsequent exercises and fill in the blanks.

16. ___Ab___ major is the relative major of ___F___ minor.

17. _____ major is the relative major of ___G___ minor.

18. _____ major is the relative major of ___Bb___ minor.

19. _____ major is the relative major of ___Ab___ minor.

20. _____ major is the relative major of ___D___ minor.

21. _____ major is the relative major of ___C___ minor.

22. _____ major is the relative major of ___A___ minor.

23. _____ major is the relative major of ___C#___ minor.

24. _____ major is the relative major of ___E___ minor.

25. _____ major is the relative major of ___G#___ minor.

26. _____ major is the relative major of ___Eb___ minor.

27. _____ major is the relative major of ___B___ minor.

28. _____ major is the relative major of ___A#___ minor.

29. _____ major is the relative major of ___D#___ minor.

30. _____ major is the relative major of ___F#___ minor.

DRILL STUDY #3

Instructions: When contrasting parallel *major* and *minor* key signatures that share the same keynote, the key signatures involved are *never* the same. In the following exercises, study the completed example (Exercise 1) carefully and fill in the remaining unknowns. Where enharmonic equivalents exist (in parenthesis), the proper responses for them should be given, as well.

PARALLEL KEY SIGNATURES

	Minor	Key Signature	Major	Key Signature
1.	G	2 ♭s	G	1 ♯
2.			B♭	
3.		3 ♯s		
4.			C♯	
5.	D			
6.		7 ♭s		
7.				No ♭s or ♯s
8.	E♭			
9.				5 ♯s
10.			F	
11.	D♯		(D♯) E♭	
12.		5 ♯s	(G♯) A♭	
13.	(D♭) C♯			
14.			E	
15.	A			
16.	(C♭) B			7 ♭s
17.		7 ♯s	(A♯) B♭	
18.	(G♭) F♯			
19.			D♭	
20.	E♭			

Instructions: In Exercises 21–40, the entire minor concept—including *parallel* and *relative*—is explored. As in all cases, and especially in cases involving enharmonic equivalents that are not shown in these exercises, it will be necessary to evaluate each factor for the proper response. Study the completed example (Exercise 21) and fill in the remaining unknowns.

| | PARALLEL | | | | |
| | RELATIVE | | | | RELATIVE | |
Minor	Same	Major	Major	Same	Minor
21. F	4♭s	A♭	F	1♭	D
22.			D		
23. G					
24.		C			
25.					G♯
26.		E♭			
27. E					
28.			C♯		
29. G♯					
30.			A♭		
31.	6♯s				
32.			F♯		
33. A♯					
34.		D♭			
35.					E♭
36.		G♭			
37.			D♭		
38.					A♭
39. C					
40.					A♯

DRILL STUDY #4

Instructions: In Exercises 1–4, in each blank set of measures, position and place the appropriate rest value under the designated bracketed note values. Play or sing each exercise individually or with a classmate in duet form. Your instructor may choose to perform these drill studies as classroom rhythmic drills or as ear-training exercises in rhythm.

Instructions: For Exercises 5–8, use the instructions to Exercises 1–4. However, *note values* as well as *rest values* are now incorporated into each drill. For each bracketed *rest* or *note value*, an *opposite equivalent value* should be placed in the blank measures provided immediately below.

ASSIGNMENT FOR CHAPTER 6

NAME _____ SCORE _____ GRADE _____

DATE DUE _____ SECTION _____ INSTRUCTOR _____

1. *Instructions:* In Parts (a)–(f), write the ascending and/or descending forms of the minor scale on the staffs provided. Be sure to alternate lines and spaces and to space the scale degrees equally for good manuscript. Provide the clef, a key signature on each staff, and any accidentals to the body of the scale.

(a) Treble Clef, A♯ Minor, Aeolian Form, Descending Only

(b) Bass Clef, B♭ Minor, Melodic Form, Ascending and Descending

(c) Alto Clef, E♭ Minor, Harmonic Form, Ascending Only

(d) Tenor Clef, D Minor, Harmonic Form, Ascending Only

(e) Treble Clef, D♯ Minor, Melodic Form, Ascending and Descending

(f) Bass Clef, A Minor, Harmonic Form, Descending Only

2. *Instructions:* In Parts (a)–(d), follow the instruction to Exercise 1 for the indicated derivative *minor scales* with their particular forms and scale directions. Provide *clefs, key signatures, accidentals,* and pay particular attention to good manuscript.

(a) C♯ Major: Treble Clef, Ascending Only

(b) Relative Minor C♯ Major: Alto Clef, Harmonic Form, Descending Only

(c) Parallel Minor C♯ Major: Tenor Clef, Melodic Form, Ascending Only

(d) Parallel Minor C♯ Major: Bass Clef, Melodic Form, Descending Only

3. *Instructions:* Correct the following poorly written measures on the blank measures provided immediately below. Assume that in each measure presented, partial or combined groupings of note and rest values are incorrectly scored and contain elements of ambiguity.

PERFORMANCE ASSIGNMENT FOR CHAPTER 6

1. *Instructions:* The following rhythm exercises are meant to prepare you for a new phase of study in music fundamentals. This very important phase is called *ear-training*.

Suggested Mode of Practice

In each exercise, study the two measure drills in the following manner:

1. Sing each exercise and give each note its full value.

2. Be sure to observe the repeat sign.

3. Listen to yourself carefully for a more profound understanding of the material.

4. After each set of drills, skip around and do the drills out of order to eliminate monotony and to heighten interest.

5. Broaden the rhythmic experience by changing tempos often.

6. After you have sung each exercise through several times, close your eyes and attempt to visualize the notation of each written expression.

(continued)

(c) (continued)

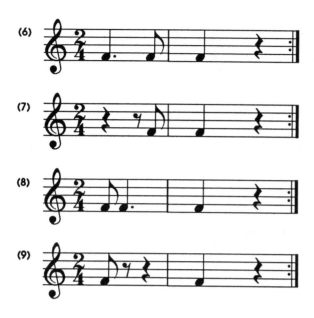

2. *Instructions:* The act of writing on paper what one hears from an outside source is described in the music classroom as *taking dictation.* The *recipient,* the one who is taking dictation, listens attentively and carefully to what is being played and reproduces on paper pitch structures and/or rhythmic invention.

Suggested Mode of Practice

The following exercises are presented as a study in dictation and are devised for two or more students or as a classroom tool for the instructor. The object of this exercise is to concentrate on the middle measure of each format presented and to write down on paper what is heard.

Each of the formats presented serves as the vehicle for the dictation process. Measures one and three will always remain constant, while the second measure—the *mystery measure*—will change with each example. Three formats are presented for study. Keep in mind that one can never hope to write as fast as a musician can play or sing; therefore, it is recommended that every attempt be made to develop one's memory. In addition, do not write while the exercise is being played; when taking dictation, every effort should be placed on concentration. Blank staves are provided for each format. Each dictation example should be given once. If a piano is used, do not use the sustaining pedal. Check your answers only when you have completed each format. Repeat this drill as many times as needed. The dictation exercises and the answers to each format are found on page 146.

Format No. 1

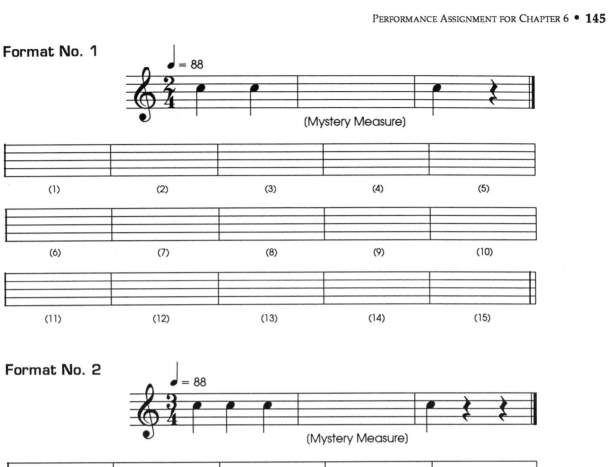

Format No. 2

Format No. 3

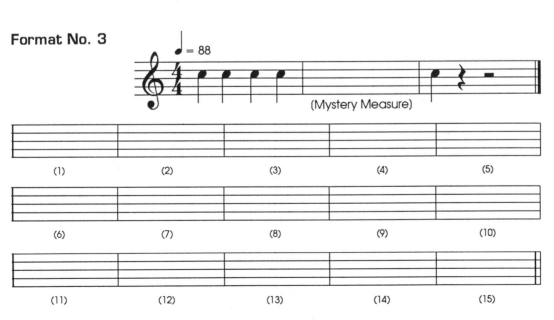

DICTATION DRILLS AND PERFORMANCE EXERCISE ANSWERS

Format No. 1

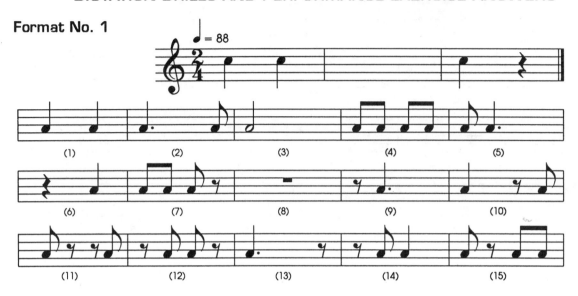

Format No. 2

Format No. 3

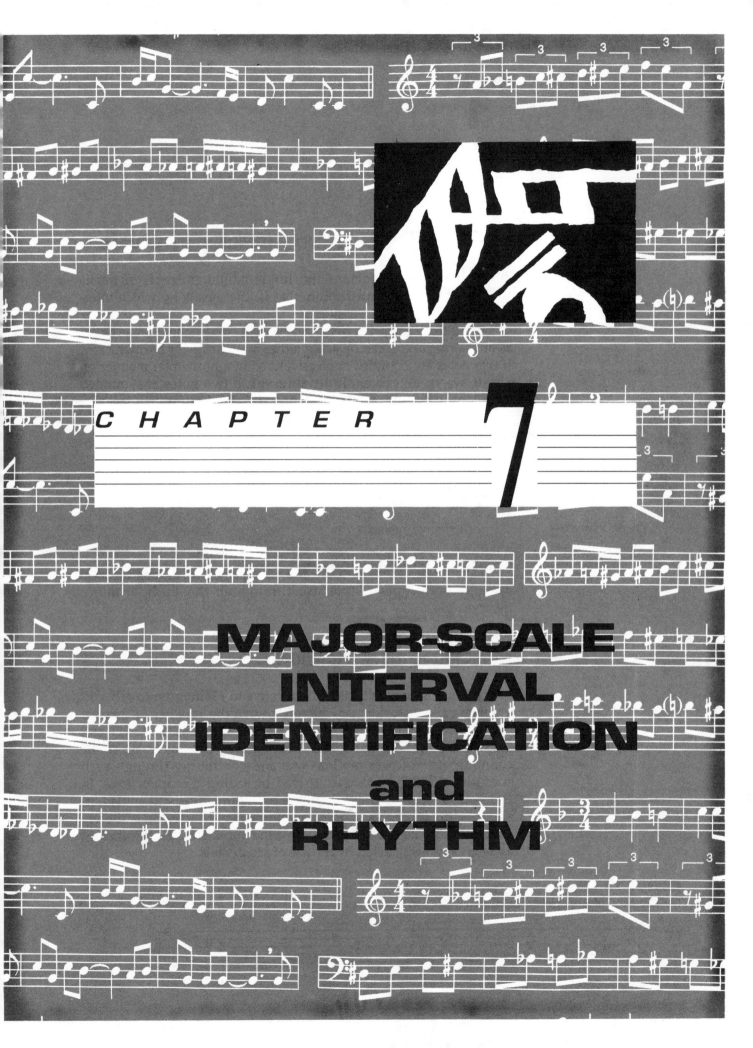

CHAPTER

7

MAJOR-SCALE
INTERVAL
IDENTIFICATION
and
RHYTHM

Section

1

Pitch Considerations

MELODIC INTERVALS AND HARMONIC INTERVALS

One of the most important and fundamental concepts of music theory is **interval identification**, that is, the means by which intervals are measured and classified.

Recall that the spatial distance between two pitches is referred to as an *interval*, and it can be heard either melodically or harmonically. If two notes are sounded successively, as in a horizontal manner on a staff, we speak of a **melodic interval**; if two notes are sounded simultaneously, as in a vertical manner, this is a **harmonic interval**.

Example 76
A melodic and a harmonic interval.

(Melodic Interval)   (Harmonic Interval)

It should be understood that the same principles of identification apply to both types of intervals throughout the study of music theory.

NUMERICAL IDENTIFICATION

Intervals are numerically measured from 1 to 13. In order to arrive at a numerical conclusion, one merely counts the number of degrees encompassed by the interval, making sure to count the lower and the upper pitches as part of the interval. The process involves the counting of the lower pitch as one and continuing through each successive line and space up to and including the upper tone. In Example 77, each set of intervals has been numerically identified. In addition, the process of arriving at a numerical conclusion is shown. Also, it should be noted carefully that the numerical identification of an interval is *not* affected by the use of accidentals.

Example 77
The numerical identification of intervals.

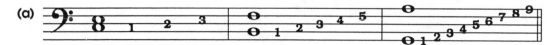

SIMPLE AND COMPOUND INTERVALS

Intervals are grouped in two ways. They may be considered *simple* or *compound*. **Simple intervals** are those with a range of one octave or less. **Compound intervals** are those with range larger than an octave. It is customary to use ordinal numbers on all of the intervals except for the Latin designated *unison* and *octave*. The term "prime" is used interchangeably with unison.

Example 78

Simple and compound intervals.

(a) Simple intervals

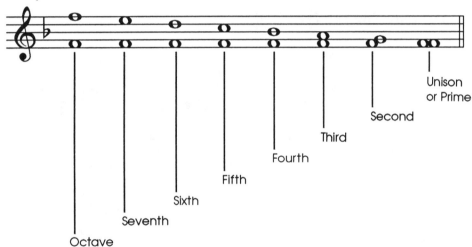

(b) Compound intervals

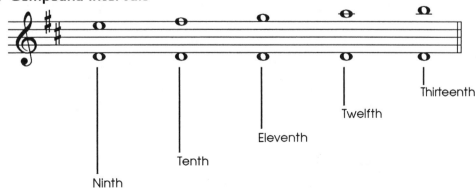

Because of certain harmonic implications, the identification of intervals larger than a thirteenth is academic and is rarely dealt with. In addition, compound intervals are often reduced by an octave and consequently are referred to as if they were in a *simple* context; for example, a ninth might be referred to as a second, a tenth as a third, an eleventh as a fourth, and so on.

Example 79
Compound intervals reduced to a simple context.

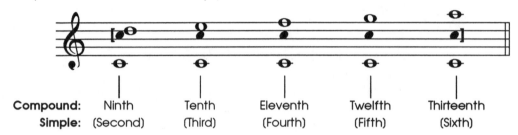

Compound:	Ninth	Tenth	Eleventh	Twelfth	Thirteenth
Simple:	(Second)	(Third)	(Fourth)	(Fifth)	(Sixth)

At this point in our study, additional terminology is needed in order to distinguish properly and identify completely the various types of intervals of the same numerical size. For that purpose it will be necessary to explore additional areas.

DIATONIC INTERVALS

The further classification of intervals requires the involvement of the diatonic major-key scheme. Through its use, **diatonic intervals** (intervals found in a major scale) are found to be grouped in two ways. They are either *perfect* or *major*, depending upon their size and position within the key scheme. It is now possible to categorize and classify intervals according to their numerical size and quality. See Table 10.

Table 10 ▪ *The Diatonic Major-Key Scheme — Perfect and Major Intervals*

(Δ9) (Δ10) (P11) (P12) (Δ13)

Perfect Octave (P8)

Major Seventh (Δ7)

Major Sixth (Δ6)

Perfect Fifth (P5)

Perfect Fourth (P4)

Major Third (Δ3)

Major Second (Δ2)

Perfect Unison (Pu) or Perfect Prime (Pp)

N.B. In this book, all major intervals will be indicated by a triangular symbol (Δ). Any reference to the letter "m" signifies a minor interval.

From the information provided in Table 10, it is safe to conclude that all *unisons* (or *primes*), *fourths* (*elevenths*), *fifths* (*twelfths*), and *octaves* are *perfect*, and all *seconds* (*ninths*), *thirds* (*tenths*), *sixths* (*thirteenths*), and *sevenths* are *major*; furthermore, when the *upper note* of the interval is in the scale of the *lower note*, the interval will always be *diatonic*. It is the key of the lower note (the **keynote**) that establishes the major key for the purpose of determining the quality of an interval. Thus, a **perfect interval** is an interval that is formed by combining the keynote of the diatonic major scale with its prime, fourth (eleventh), fifth (twelfth), or octave degrees. A **major interval** is an interval that is formed by combining the keynote of the diatonic major scale with its second (ninth), third (tenth), sixth (thirteenth), and seventh degrees.

Study carefully the following sets of intervals; they have all been completely identified.

Example 80
Diatonic major-scale intervals with key signatures.

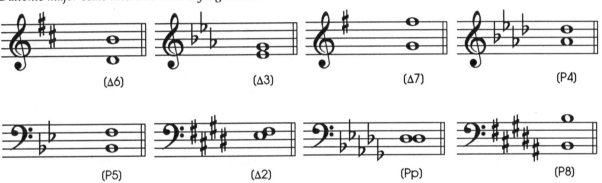

In Example 81, key signatures are not provided, and yet the intervals are completely identifiable. The reason for this—and it is worth repeating—is that in each instance, the upper note is found in the scale or tonality of the all-important bottom note. Although both notes are needed to evaluate the quality and numerical value of an interval, it is the bottom note that is used to determine if, indeed, the interval belongs to a diatonic major-key scheme. The following set of intervals is presented *without* key signatures.

Example 81
Diatonic major-scale intervals without key signatures.

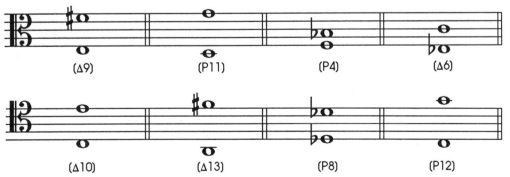

Section
2

The Notation of Rhythm

COMPOUND TIME

Thus far, our discussion of rhythm has involved *simple meter* (or *simple time*), with its subdivision of the beat (pulse) into two equal parts and the various concepts that relate to its notation. At this point of our study, we will explore the many facets of another common rhythmic concept, namely, *compound meter* (*compound time*).

THE UNIT OF MEASURE IN COMPOUND TIME

While some of the notational concepts learned in simple time are shared with compound meter, the unit of measure (the beat or pulse) in *compound time* is subdivided into three equal parts and is markedly different in performance than in *simple time*. For instance, *simple duple* gives a feeling of two beats per measure, with each beat equally divided. On the other hand, *compound duple* is also performed with two beats per measure; however, a primary difference between the two rhythmic ideas exists in performance, where compound time is equally divided into three parts, instead of two.

Sing and practice the following comparative example. You will notice that in *simple time*, the eighth-note value receives one-half of a beat, while the eighth-note value in *compound time* receives one-third of a beat. Because they are to be performed in both simple duple and compound duple, they will each receive two beats to the measure. For the purposes of performance, pay particular attention to the metronome markings. Notice that the unit of measure in *compound time* is given as a dotted quarter note. In point of fact, all units of measure in *compound time* are *always* shown as dotted note values.

Example 82
Simple duple vs. compound duple.

(a) Simple Duple

(b) Compound Duple

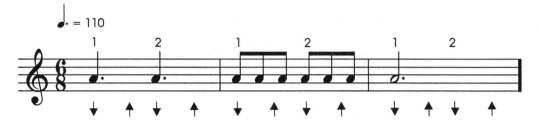

COMPOUND-TIME SIGNATURES

Compound-time signatures are traditionally found in three separate categories; they can be classified as *compound duple* (meaning two beats to the measure), *compound triple* (meaning three beats to the measure), or *compound quadruple* (meaning four beats to the measure). Time signatures beyond these three categories exist, but are seldom seen in the literature. Table 11 presents some of the possible time signatures found in the aforementioned categories.

DETERMINING THE MODE OF PERFORMANCE

While all *compound-time* signatures can be performed in *simple time* by doing what the time signature purports to say, they are, for the most part, performed in a *compound* manner. If specific time signatures can be interpreted in two possible ways, how does one determine the correct mode of performance? The answer to this all-important question is twofold. In the first instance, all *compound-time* signatures have one thing in common. As is presented in Table 11, all of the numerators—6, 9, and 12—are (equally) divisible by three. Randomly selected time signatures with numerators that are not divisible by three do not function as compound-time signatures. Therefore, compound-time signatures with numerators of 1, 2, 4, 5, 7, 8, 10, and 11 are not possible. Although a numerator of three is

Table 11 ▪ *Compound-Time Categories*				
COMPOUND DUPLE				
6/2	6/4	6/8	6/16	6/32
COMPOUND TRIPLE				
9/2	9/4	9/8	9/16	9/32
COMPOUND QUADRUPLE				
12/2	12/4	12/8	12/16	12/32

clearly divisible by 3, it is *never* considered a compound-time signature, nor is it part of the general concept. Compound-time signatures begin with numerators of six and continue on in multiples of three.

Descriptive language terms or specific metronome markings placed at the beginning of a composition serve as the second means of determining the mode of performance. A descriptive language term such as **allegro vivace**, which indicates to the performer a certain degree of urgency and speed, would hardly be conducted in a fast six, nine, or twelve beats to the measure. On the other hand, the term **largo**, which tells the performer to play very slowly, would *not* be used to indicate two, three, or four beats to the measure when a *simple-time* interpretation would be more conducive. When a composition with a *compound-time* signature and a descriptive language term indicating a fast tempo is given, the composition will be performed most often in a *compound* manner. The opposite is true of a slower tempo composition; it would most often be performed in a *simple* manner. Metronome markings, on the other hand, are very clear. As was stated earlier, all metronome markings involving a *compound* interpretation of a composition are indicated with a dotted note value at the very beginning of the composition.

Example 83
Contrasting simple and compound interpretation.

Simple

Compound triple

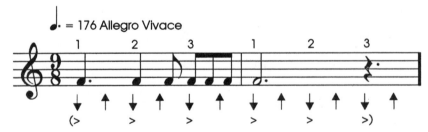

The materials presented concerning the mode of performance provide a means of interpreting metronome markings, which are the descriptive language terms used for tempo designations, for time signatures, as well as for how the measure is divided, and for perhaps the most important aspect of *compound* time, how the pulse or beat is subdivided. One additional aspect of performance remains. In order to feel the subdivision of the beat in comparing *simple* versus *compound*, return to Example 83 and observe the placement of accent marks. Singing, hearing, and comparing the sound should provide a clearer understanding of how each beat is subdivided. Be sure to emphasize the accented notes.

GROUPING IN COMPOUND METER

One of the most important notational concepts connected with compound meter is proper *grouping*. It was previously introduced in the discussion of simple time; it is another concept shared between simple and compound rhythm.

In order to have proper grouping in the notating of compound meter, just make certain that each compound beat contains a grouping of three, as determined by the denominator of the time signature. For example, if a composition is written in $\frac{6}{8}$ time, the value of what is placed in a one-beat grouping must *not* exceed the value of three eighth notes. Or, in other words, a grouping of note values in one beat in a compound-time signature cannot exceed that of its unit value (that is, the *beat*).

Equal division does play a role in compound time and is another concept shared in rhythm; however, it is only applied to compound quadruple time.

Example 84
Proper grouping in compound meter.

Finally, the following notion must be adhered to whenever writing music in compound time. Although it is possible to interpret music written with a compound-time signature in simple or compound time, it must always be written as if it is to be performed in a compound manner. Study the following mixed groupings, and be sure to relate them to the time signatures given.

Example 85
Proper grouping in compound quadruple meter.

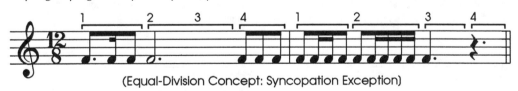

(Equal-Division Concept: Syncopation Exception)

THE USE OF REST VALUES IN COMPOUND METER

It was stated that in simple time rest values were, for the most part, never dotted. In compound time, the opposite is true. Partial rest values within beats and in combination with note values are written according to context and may or may not use dots. However, complete rest beats and consolidated rest values are dotted. Rest values may even exist within beamed groupings and, in fact, are strongly recommended for ease of reading.

Example 86
The use of rest values in compound groupings.

One very important convention concerning rest values is the use of partial rests. This notion states that if the first third or fraction thereof of the last beat of any compound measure is occupied by a note value and if the last two-thirds are rested, then the rested portion of the final beat must be individually rested according to the denominator of the time signature. Consolidation of partial beats in other parts of the measure, however, is recommended. One final admonition! Because compound-time signatures must be written in a compound manner, any written measure that appears to be in simple time will essentially be wrong.

Three sets of representative measures are presented for study. Compare each measure and read carefully each explanation placed under the ambiguous and recommended solutions.

Example 87
Solutions to rest values in compound groupings.

(a)

(Ambiguous)

(Recommended)

The notation is incorrect. The measure appears as simple triple. Also, the grouping is muddled by the eighth-note beam. The first two-thirds of beat one is not consolidated.

The flagged eighth notes and the consolidated quarter-rest value help maintain the integrity of the grouping. The appearance of the measure is compound duple.

(b)

(Ambiguous)

(Recommended)

This measure appears to be in simple triple time. The first beat lacks consolidation.

Consolidating the first beat helps to maintain the integrity of the compound-grouping process.

(c)

(Ambiguous)

This measure appears to be written in simple triple time. The beaming of the eighth notes in the middle of the measure further complicates the issue and prevents the proper notating of this compound meter.

(Recommended)

Eliminating the beam on the flagged eighth-note values helps to define the compound grouping process. Eighth rest values that are individually rested adhere to the "last two-thirds rule" for compound meters.

MANUSCRIPT TIPS

The notating of two sounds that are struck or sounded simultaneously demands some attention. When scoring an interval of the second, it is important to score the second in a diagonal fashion—diagonally to the right and up, making sure that both note heads touch, but do not overlap. All other intervals, exclusive of accidentals, are not a problem and are aligned regularly in a vertical manner.

Notating rules that govern the traditional placement of accidentals before note heads in the alignment of intervals, and especially seconds through sixths, are standard. There are few exceptions. Traditionally, the accidental governing the upper note is placed closer to the note head, while the one affecting the bottom note is placed diagonally to the left. All intervals that are larger than a sixth have their respective accidentals aligned in a perpendicular fashion.

Example 88
The traditional placement of accidentals.

Manuscript Practice

Use these manuscript pages for note taking and drill.

DRILL STUDY #1

Quiz

Instructions: In Exercises 1–10, fill in the blanks. [Quiz answers are provided at the bottom of the page.]

1. The quality of a diatonic interval can only be _____ or _____ , depending upon its size.

2. All diatonic unisons (or primes), fourths, fifths, and octaves are _____ .

3. Intervals such as ninths, tenths, elevenths, twelfths, and thirteenths are classified as

   _____ .

4. All diatonic seconds, thirds, sixths, and sevenths are _____ .

5. Numerical identification of an interval is not affected by the use of _____ .

6. All diatonic ninths, tenths, and thirteenths are _____ .

7. When the upper note is in the _____ of the lower note, the interval will always be diatonic.

8. All diatonic elevenths and twelfths are _____ .

9. Intervals that are an octave or smaller in size are classified as _____ .

10. Numerically speaking, an octave plus a third would add up to a _____ .

11. *Instructions:* As in the first measure, identify numerically each of the following intervals in the brackets provided below. Be sure to count the lower and upper notes as part of the interval. Also, encircle the classification letters S or C, representing simple or compound, respectively, below each interval.

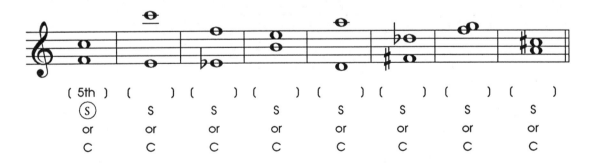

QUIZ ANSWERS:

1. *perfect, major* 2. *perfect* 3. *compound* 4. *major* 5. *accidentals* 6. *major* 7. *scale* 8. *perfect* 9. *simple* 10. *tenth*

12. *Instructions:* As in the first measure of Part (a), identify the following diatonic intervals as to size and quality in the brackets provided below. Be sure to use the bottom note of each interval as the keynote of the key and encircle the classification letters S or C, representing simple or compound, respectively, below each interval. Refer to the chapter as often as is necessary.

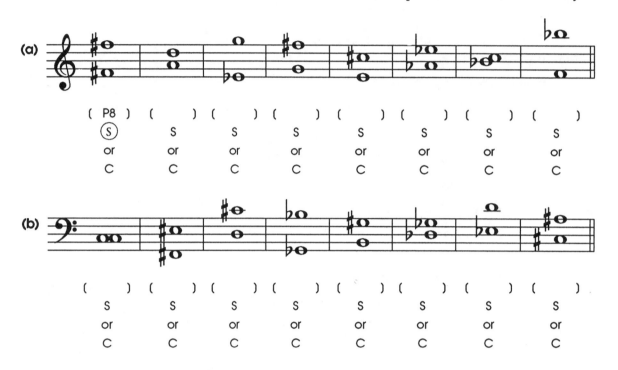

13. *Instructions:* As in the first measure, below each interval supply the upper note above each given pitch according to the desired interval and, in addition, classify each interval by encircling the representative letter S or C, as simple or compound, respectively. Refer to the chapter as often as is necessary.

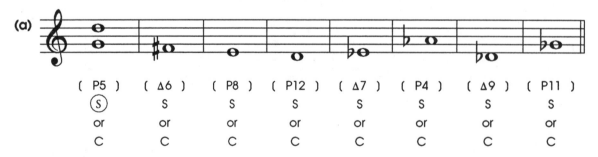

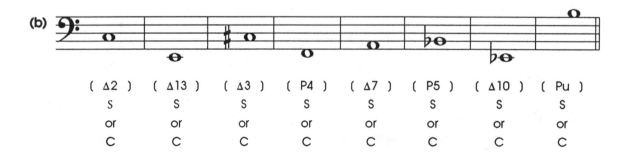

DRILL STUDY #2

1. *Instructions:* In Parts (b)–(f), supply the missing information on the blanks provided adjacent to each time signature. Identify the meter using the correct terminology as it relates to the numerator, and indicate the note value that receives the unit of measure on the lower line adjacent to the denominator. See the model in Part (a).

(a) $\frac{6}{8}$ _____ compound duple _____
a dotted quarter note

(d) $\frac{12}{8}$ _____

(b) $\frac{9}{16}$ _____

(e) $\frac{9}{4}$ _____

(c) $\frac{6}{4}$ _____

(f) $\frac{6}{16}$ _____

2. *Instructions:* In each of the following rhythmic excerpts, determine the note value that represents the unit of measure. Then indicate measures by placing bar lines in the appropriate places. After you have completed the exercises, it is highly recommended that you sing them individually or as a classroom drill. You may even choose to play them on the piano or any other instrument.

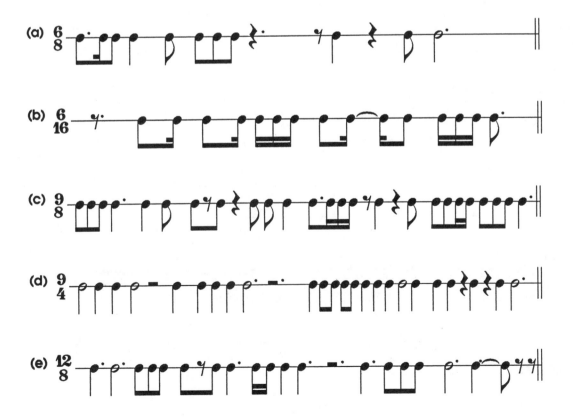

3. *Instructions:* On the blank measures provided in each part, write the correct notation for the given compound meter. Assume that each example given is incorrectly scored and needs proper grouping. Refer to the chapter as often as is necessary. Again, as in Exercise 2, perform each corrected excerpt.

ASSIGNMENT FOR CHAPTER 7

NAME _____ SCORE _____ GRADE _____

DATE DUE _____ SECTION _____ INSTRUCTOR _____

1. *Instructions:* As in Part (a), identify diatonic intervals in Parts (b)–(f) in the brackets provided below each interval.

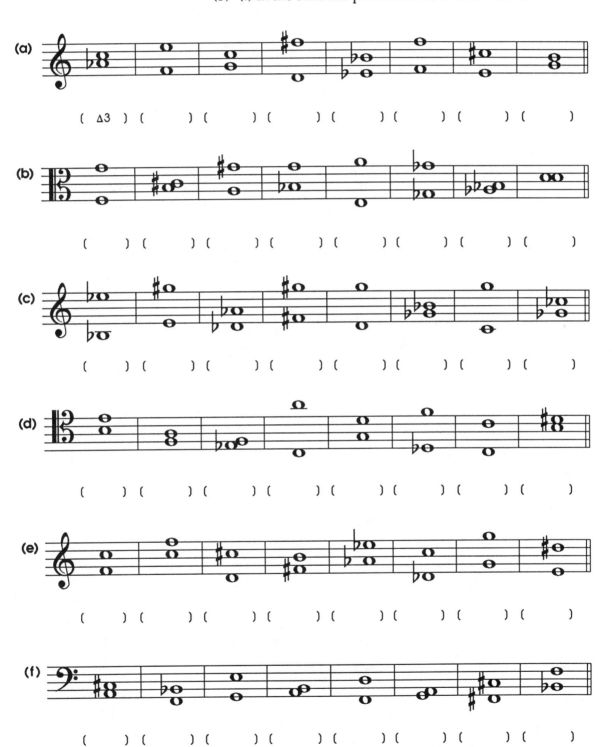

2. *Instructions:* Supply the missing upper note of the following diatonic intervals. Be sure that the upper note is found in the scale and major key of the lower note.

(Δ6)　(Δ7)　(P4)　(P5)　(Δ7)　(Δ2)　(Δ3)　(P5)

(Δ7)　(Δ3)　(P4)　(Δ7)　(P11)　(Δ6)　(P4)　(Δ9)

3. *Instructions:* Supply the missing lower note of the following diatonic intervals. Be sure that both notes of the interval are found in the scale and major key of the lower note.

(P5)　(Δ3)　(Δ6)　(Δ9)　(P4)　(Δ2)　(Δ6)　(Δ7)

(P11)　(Δ7)　(P8)　(Δ13)　(P4)　(Δ2)　(Δ3)　(Δ2)

4. *Instructions:* In the following rhythmic excerpts, determine the note value that represents the unit of measure and place the bar lines in the appropriate places. Assume that these excerpts are to be performed in a compound manner.

PERFORMANCE ASSIGNMENT FOR CHAPTER 7

1. *Instructions:* The material in this assignment is meant to be used for sight singing and ear training.

Suggested Mode of Practice

The performance symbol (⌢) is called a **fermata**; it is used in written music to indicate a prolonged sound or silence of indefinite time. It is used here to help establish tonal memory along with the short-pause symbol (//). Begin these exercises by sounding a middle c on the piano or on a pitch pipe. Using **solfeggio** (vocal exercises sung to a system of designated degrees of the scale by syllables (do–re–, etc.), rather than by letters), sing and sustain the second pitch of the interval as indicated, while listening and carefully attempting to register the interval's sound in your memory. These exercises in ear training are intended either for individual study or else for use as a classroom tool. One caution! If you use the piano, use it only to monitor your pitch *after* you've sung the interval, *not* before.

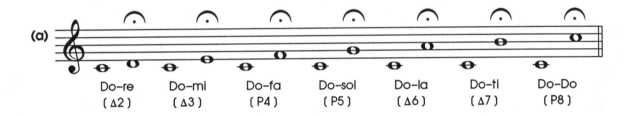

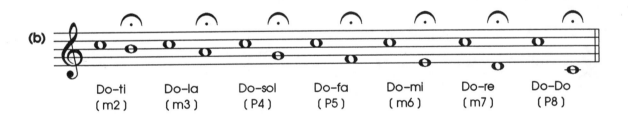

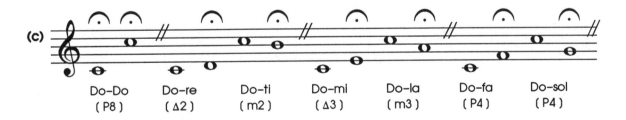

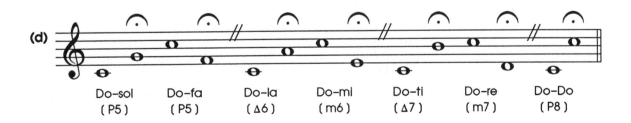

2. *Instructions:* The ability to sight sing intervals and to identify them is of paramount importance to the aspiring musician. In this part of the assignment, the melodic material presented is taken from Exercise 1 and involves an attempt to strengthen tonal memory through the use of diatonic intervals found within the major tonality.

Suggested Mode of Practice

In the pursuit of developing a fine ear, only twelve intervals need be involved for study. Thus far, we have presented eleven intervals and they are as follows: m2, Δ2, m3, Δ3, P4, P5, m6, Δ6, m7, Δ7, and P8. We have achieved this number by presenting study drills in ascending and descending form as they relate to the diatonic major scale. The following materials should be sung and used for dictation purposes. The most effective way to utilize these drills in dictation is to use partial measures. Use the piano as in Exercise 1, and choose various tempos of performance. Again, these drills are meant for individual and small-group study, but they may also be used as a classroom tool by the instructor.

THREE MELODIES

(a) Seconds and Thirds

(b) Fourths, Fifths, and a Special Fourth*

(c) Sixths, Sevenths, and Octaves

---

*A special fourth, as used in Part (b), will be identified and discussed in Chapters 8 and 9.

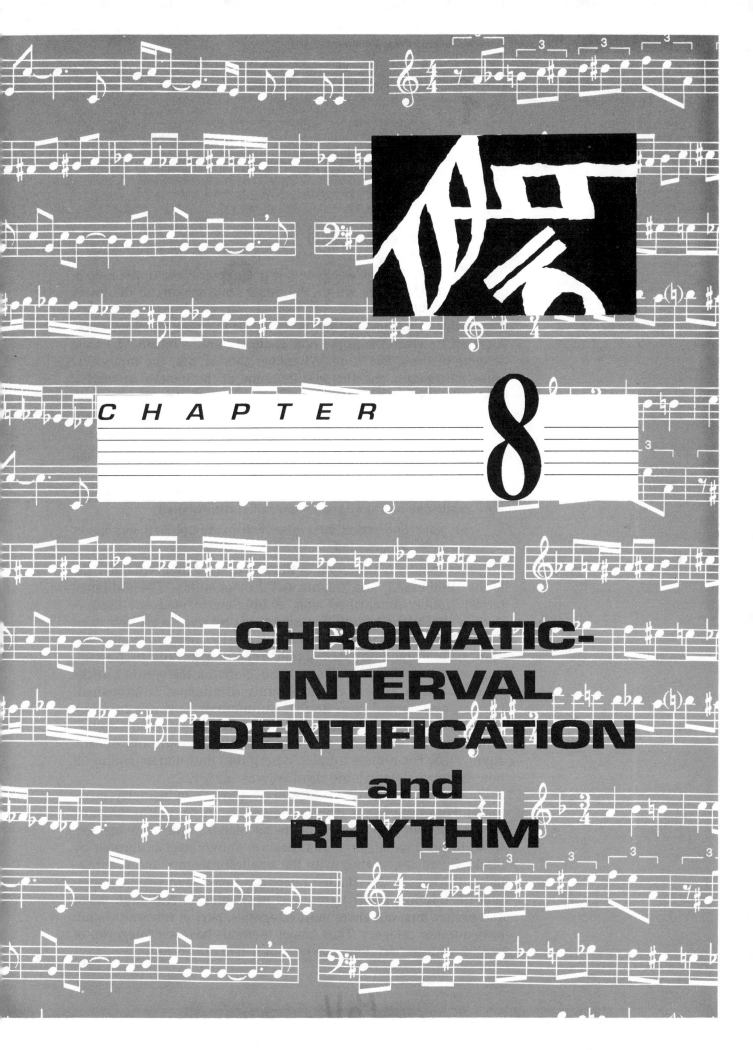

CHAPTER

8

CHROMATIC-
INTERVAL
IDENTIFICATION
and
RHYTHM

Section

1

Pitch Considerations

CHROMATIC INTERVALS

In the discussion of *diatonic* intervals in Chapter 7, the upper note of the interval had to be within the major-scale scheme of the lower note. When this ocurred, the interval was either *major* or *perfect*, depending upon its size and scale location. Now consider those intervals in which the upper note is altered and is outside the scale scheme of the lower tone. Whenever this occurs, the interval is called **chromatic**, and the specific name of the interval created is changed accordingly.

- All *major* intervals when made one half step smaller are called **minor**.
- All *minor* intervals when made one half step smaller are called **diminished**.
- All *perfect* intervals, with the exception of the unison, when made one half step smaller are called **diminished**.
- All *major* and *perfect* intervals when made one half step larger are called **augmented**.

Occasionally, an interval is altered to an extent whereby the terms "diminished" and "augmented" do not suffice. The additional terms, "doubly diminished" and "doubly augmented" are used. A **doubly diminished (doubly augmented) interval** is a diminished (an augmented) interval that is made smaller (larger) by one half step. It must be emphasized that unisons can only be perfect, augmented, and doubly augmented. Fourths (elevenths), fifths (twelfths), and octaves can be doubly diminished, diminished, perfect, augmented, and doubly augmented. Seconds (ninths), thirds (tenths), sixths (thirteenths), and sevenths can become doubly diminished, diminished, minor, major, augmented, and doubly augmented. For a more graphic description and understanding of how chromatic intervals are classified, see Table 12.

In Table 12, altered intervals are categorized by half-step increments. For example, the distance between a minor and major category is one half step. All others are calculated in the same manner. In addition, the category qualities are shown and calibrated by blackened circles, starting with the smallest category and progressing to the largest. The shaded categories (major and perfect) represent the diatonic levels introduced in Chapter 7. Although major and perfect intervals share most categories, perfect intervals do not have a minor category. Thus, major intervals have six categories of quality, while perfect intervals have only five categories.

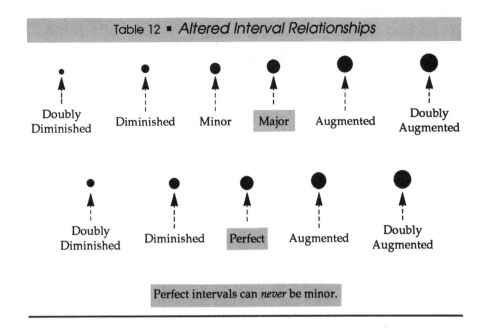

Table 12 ▪ *Altered Interval Relationships*

Perfect intervals can *never* be minor.

The following intervals should be thoroughly understood before proceeding to new material. Study them carefully. Also, in this textbook, the smaller-dimensional intervals are indicated in lower case, whereas upper-case letters are reserved for the contrasting larger-dimensional intervals.

Example 89
Altered intervals.

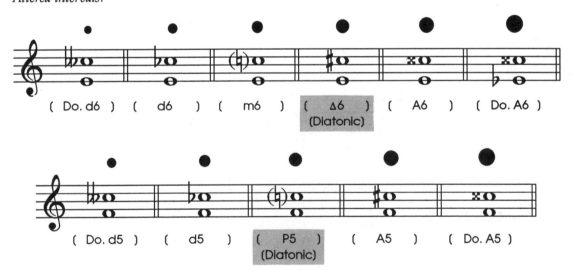

INTERVAL INVERSION

At this point in our study, no additional information is needed to identify completely any interval that one might encounter. However, there remains one aspect of interval identification that is worth mentioning. This is the involvement of **inversion**, as described in Tables 13 and 14 on page 172, which should be studied carefully. This

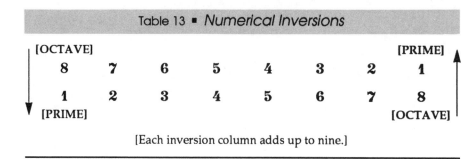

Table 13 ■ *Numerical Inversions*

[OCTAVE]							[PRIME]
8	7	6	5	4	3	2	1
1	2	3	4	5	6	7	8
[PRIME]							[OCTAVE]

[Each inversion column adds up to nine.]

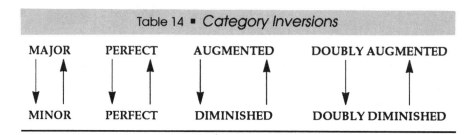

Table 14 ■ *Category Inversions*

MAJOR	PERFECT	AUGMENTED	DOUBLY AUGMENTED
MINOR	PERFECT	DIMINISHED	DOUBLY DIMINISHED

concept allows for a flexibility and for a means of identifying difficult or rarely seen intervals more rapidly. Also, it may be used for checking or verifying answers.

The following sets of intervals contain inverted numerical and category inversions. They are completely identified.

Example 90
Inverted intervals.

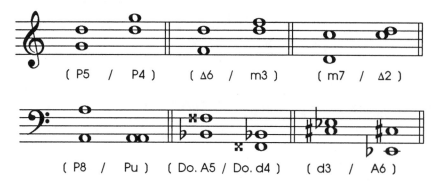

Each interval in Example 91 has been completely identified and has been presented with its individual solution. Often, more than one approach is both possible and necessary in order to identify an interval adequately; therefore, in most cases, a combination of references is given.

Study each example carefully before proceeding to the drill sheets provided at the end of this chapter.

Example 91

Chromatic and diatonic intervals.

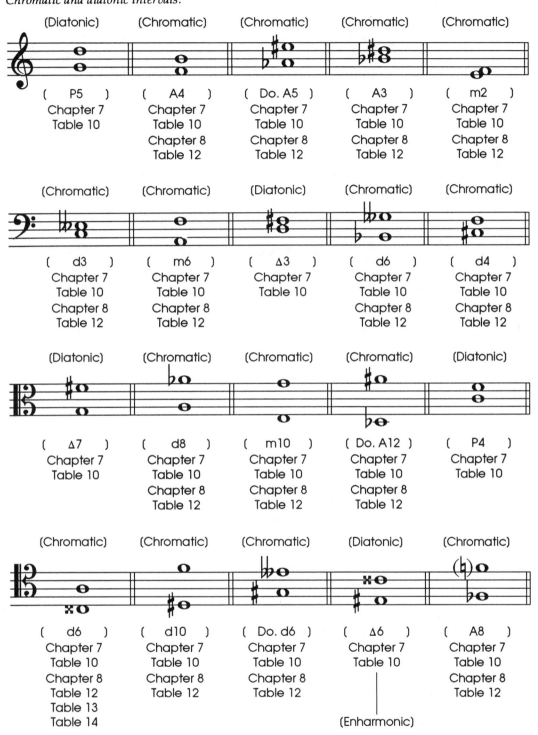

INTERVALS OF ENHARMONIC EQUIVALENCY

Finally, intervals can be linked enharmonically and can sound the same, yet be called by different names—depending upon the context of the music. For example, an augmented prime (Ap) and a doubly diminished third (Do. d3) both sound the same as a minor second (m2); an augmented third (A3) and a perfect fourth (P4) both sound the same as a doubly diminished fifth (Do. d5); an augmented fourth (A4) sounds the same as a diminished fifth (d5); a minor seventh (m7) and a doubly diminished octave (Do. d8) both sound the same as an augmented sixth (A6). Of course, there are many more such examples. The determination of what is actually heard depends, in large measure, on the context of the musical passage and on a thorough understanding of music theory.

Study the following interval table of enharmonic equivalents. Only the more practical combinations are presented.

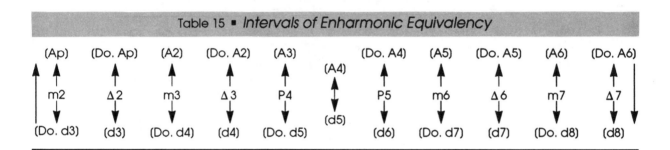

Table 15 ▪ *Intervals of Enharmonic Equivalency*

Section

2

The Notation of Rhythm

The notating of unequal rhythmic groupings within a *meter* (measurement) is an especially perplexing problem for the musician. The borrowing of note values or particular groupings from compound time and inserting and subdividing them into simple time, or vice versa, further complicates the picture. All of these matters are linked together; they necessarily involve the complete understanding of meter, the normal division of the beat and its subdivision.

BORROWED DIVISION

Often, in simple time, a note is subdivided as if it were part of a compound expression. This change of subdivision and its placement is referred to as **borrowed division**. It is the act of borrowing a rhythmic grouping from compound meter and placing it, momentarily, in a simple-time environment, or vice versa. This change of normal division is not a rare occurrence, but, rather, a device that is heard and experienced very often. The most common instance of borrowed division in music—and it occurs most often in simple time—is the placement of a compound grouping called a *triplet* into simple time. A **triplet** is a three-note grouping found in compound meter in which the subdivision is normally in three. A **duplet**, on the other hand, a common two-note grouping in *simple* time in which the subdivision is normally in two, is sometimes placed in a compound environment.

Example 92 shows the use of borrowed division with duplets and triplets. Study this example carefully.

Example 92
Borrowed division with duplets and triplets.

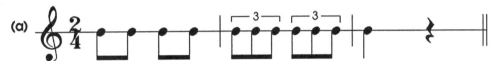

This musical expression is in simple-duple time with each beat of the first measure normally subdivided in two. Each beat of the second measure, however, is borrowed from compound time and, momentarily, is subdivided in three.

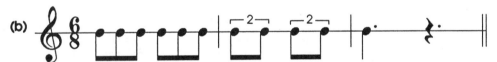

This musical expression is in compound-duple time with each beat of the first measure normally subdivided in three. Each beat of the second measure, however, is borrowed from simple time and, momentarily, is subdivided in two.

THE PERFORMANCE OF TRIPLETS AND DUPLETS

Knowing how to perform note-value groupings involving borrowed division is predicated on understanding a single statement of direction. In simple time, all borrowed note-value groupings of three must always be performed in the time of two, where the note values are of the same quality. As in Example 93, a three eighth-note grouping is performed in the time of two eighth notes; a quarter-note grouping of three in the time of two quarter notes; and a grouping of three half notes in the time of two half notes.

Example 93

Triplet note-value grouping in simple time.

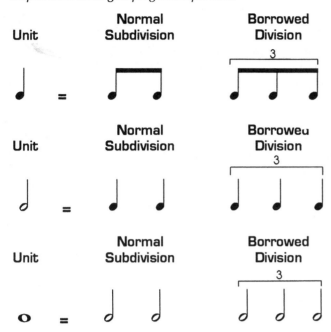

As previously stated, the performance of borrowed-division groupings in simple time is a matter of simply sounding a three-note grouping in the time of two, where the note values are of the same quality. Compound groupings of two, on the other hand, work in the opposite fashion. Their performance is predicated on the playing of a grouping of two in the time of three, where, again, the note values are of the same quality. Thus, a grouping of two eighth notes would be performed in the time of three eighth notes, and a grouping of two quarter notes would be performed in the time of three quarter notes. Unlike simple time, only two duplet note-value groupings are commonly found in compound time; they are presented in Example 94.

Example 94

Duplet note-value groupings in compound time.

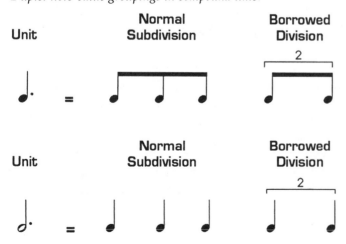

The mixture of borrowed-division note groupings in simple and compound time represents creative, rhythmic interest at its best; however, overuse of this device in a musical selection can be poor, boring, and monotonous. If used sparingly and in a very judicious manner, it can be extremely effective.

MANUSCRIPT TIPS

In the writing of borrowed-division groupings that do not contain beams, the placement or absence of a number or bracket is critical. The use of the number is critical for it informs the performer of the ensuing, unusual subdivision about to take place. The bracket (sometimes drawn as an arc) is necessary, except for eighth-note groupings, for it groups together those particular notes that belong to the triplet or duplet figure. For instance, in a quarter-note grouping in which no beam is used, the bracket ensures readability and clearly outlines and groups the necessary notes for the triplet or duplet.

Groupings found in single-line music usually place the number and bracket, if used, closest to the beam and opposite to the note heads; however, as a reminder, the direction of the stems and beams is predicated on the position of the note heads on the staff. In other words, numbers and brackets are often found placed next to note heads in various groupings.

Example 95
Triplet note-value groupings.

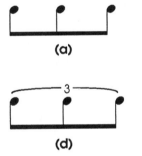

(a)

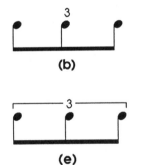

(b)

(c)

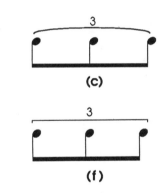

(d)

(e)

(f)

(a) This grouping is found most often in compound time, but is also allowed in simple time. Because the beaming helps define the grouping, the number and bracket are not necessary. However, borrowed groupings of quarter notes or half notes, which do not have beams, require a number and a bracket in simple as well as in compound time.

(b) This grouping is found in simple time and does not contain a bracket. Again, the bracket is not necessary because the beaming defines the grouping. Groupings of longer note values, such as quarter or half notes, necessitate the use of numbers as well as brackets.

(c) This grouping utilizes an arc instead of a bracket. In addition, notice that the number is stylistically placed above the arc.

(d) This grouping is used and is referred to as a "**triplet with the number intersecting its arc.**" Both examples (c) and (d) are commonly found in music literature in eighth-note groupings.

(e) In this grouping the number intersects the bracket; the grouping is used a great deal of the time.

(f) In this grouping the number is placed above the bracket and is, perhaps, the most clearly defined triplet figure.

The placement of the number is very precise. It is always placed directly above or below the *central element in time* of a grouping of three, *not* the central element of the grouping. In the grouping of two even or uneven elements, the number is placed directly between the two note heads and slightly above or below the level of each note head, depending upon the direction of the stems.

Example 96
The central element in time.

(a)   (b)   (c)   (d)

(a) This eighth-note triplet is drawn incorrectly because the number 3 is placed above the middle element of the grouping.

(b) In this example, the eighth-note triplet is drawn correctly because the number 3 is placed above the *central element in time* of the grouping.

(c) and **(d)** In any grouping of two elements, the number is placed directly between the two note heads.

If the elements within the borrowed groupings are further subdivided, rested, or combined, the rules concerning the placement of the number and the bracket remain the same. In Example 97, line (a) is commonly found in compound time; line (b) involves borrowed division, but is also commonly found in simple time; line (c) is a modern refinement that utilizes the beam as a grouping device. Although line (c) is not often seen in traditional manuscript, it is acceptable in both simple and compound time. A number and/or a bracket may be added to each grouping.

Example 97
Acceptable subdivision in simple and compound time.

(a)

(b)

(c)

Manuscript Practice

Use these manuscript pages for note taking and drill.

DRILL STUDY #1

Instructions: In Exercises 1–3, provide an augmented and doubly augmented interval for each major interval given. In each group, supply the upper note of the interval. Be sure to refer to the chapter as often as is necessary.

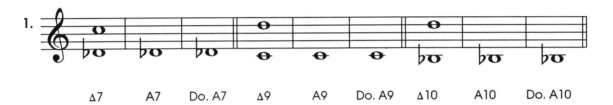

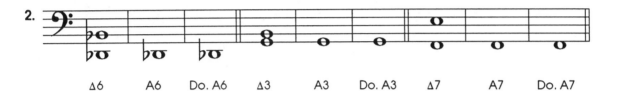

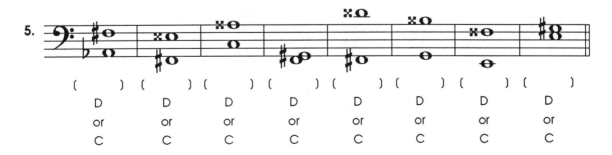

Instructions: As in the first instance in Exercise 4, identify the following mixture of diatonic and chromatic intervals given in Exercises 4 and 5. Refer to both Chapters 7 and 8, on intervals, as often as is necessary.

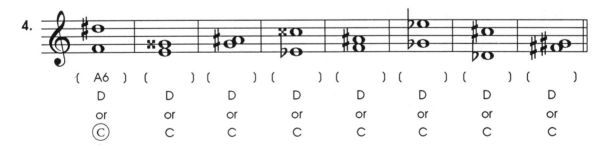

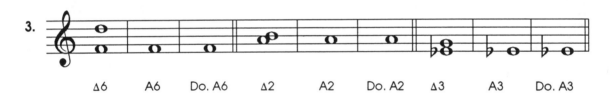

Instructions: In each group of intervals in Exercises 6–8, provide the upper note of the designated interval. Notice how each grouping is presented. The larger, major interval is placed to the right to help you gain a better understanding of the incremental variation of intervals in each grouping.

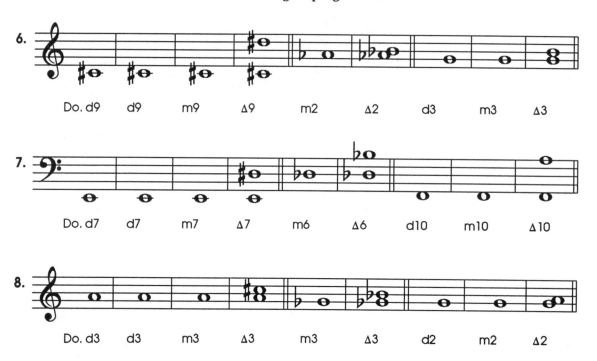

Instructions: Below each interval identify within the brackets provided and encircle the appropriate letter designation for the mixtures of diatonic and chromatic intervals presented in Exercises 9 and 10.

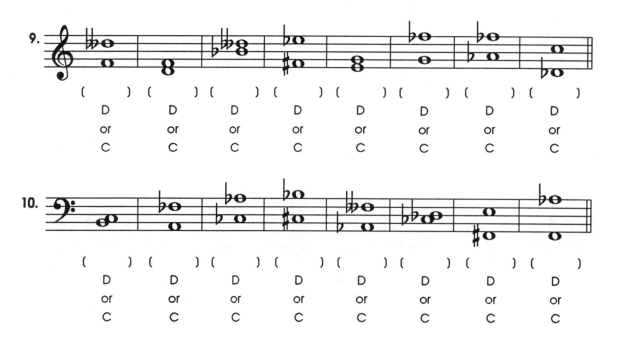

DRILL STUDY #2

Instructions: Provide an augmented and doubly augmented interval for each perfect interval given in Exercises 1–3. In each group, supply the upper note of the interval. Be sure to refer to the chapter as often as is necessary; in addition, review the incremental variations of intervals.

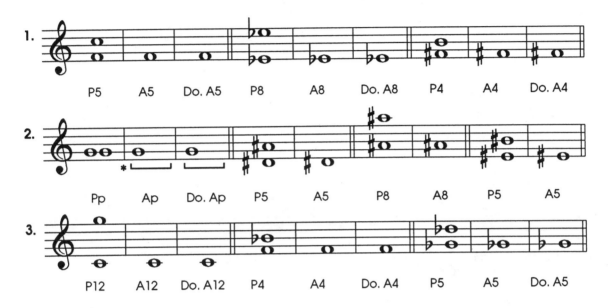

Instructions: Below each interval, identify and encircle the appropriate letter designation for the mixture of diatonic and chromatic intervals presented in Exercises 4 and 5. Refer to both Chapters 6 and 7, on intervals, as often as is necessary.

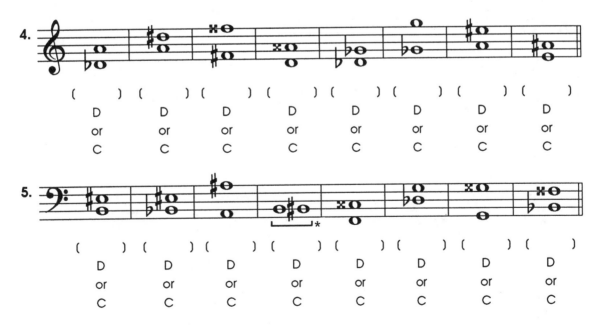

*When an altered prime interval is to be played vertically, a bracket should be placed under or above the interval for clarity of performance.

Instructions: In each group of intervals in Exercises 6–8, provide the upper note of the designated interval. The largest, perfect interval is presented to the right in each grouping to help ensure a better understanding of incremental variation and size of intervals.

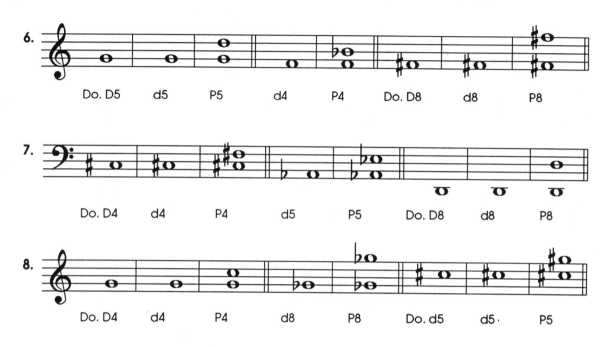

Instructions: Below each interval identify within the brackets provided and encircle the appropriate letter designation for the mixture of diatonic and chromatic intervals presented in Exercises 9 and 10.

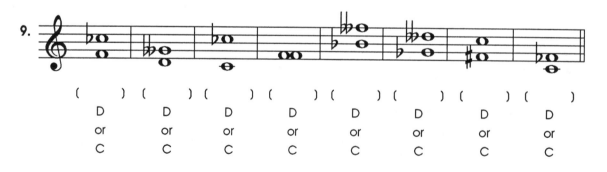

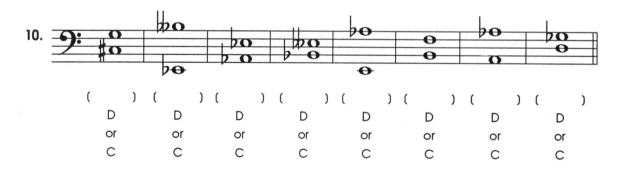

DRILL STUDY #3

Instructions: Supply the missing upper note to the diatonic and chromatic intervals given in Exercises 1–5. Again, refer to Chapters 6 and 7 as often as is necessary.

1.

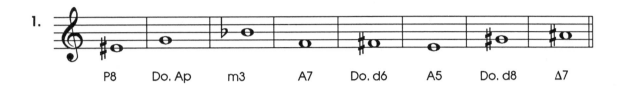

P8   Do. Ap   m3   A7   Do. d6   A5   Do. d8   Δ7

2.

Ap   m2   d3   A3   d4   d8   Do. A6   d5

3.

m6   P4   Δ3   Do. A4   Δ6   A8   m7   A2

4.

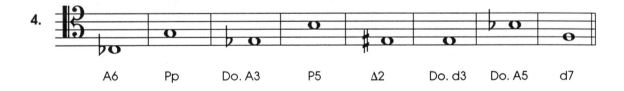

A6   Pp   Do. A3   P5   Δ2   Do. d3   Do. A5   d7

5.

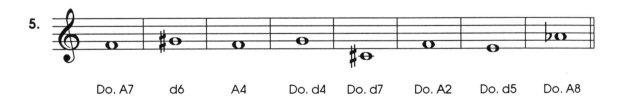

Do. A7   d6   A4   Do. d4   Do. d7   Do. A2   Do. d5   Do. A8

Instructions: Exercises 6–9 test your comprehension of interval inversion. Notate the inversion of each interval; also, identify the original and the inverted interval in the brackets provided immediately below.

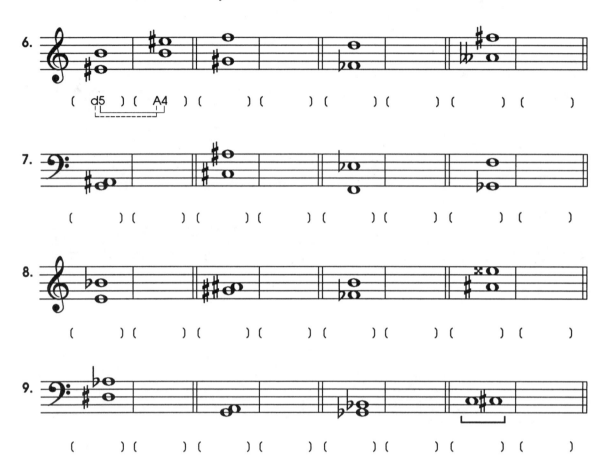

Instructions: In each of the blank brackets in Exercises 10–19, supply the missing enharmonic equivalents. Attempt to visualize the keyboard, your instrument, or the staff as you work through Exercises 10–19.

Enharmonic Equivalents

	I		II		III		I		II		III
10. (	A2	) (		) (		)	**15.** (	Δ2	) (		) (		)
11. (		) (		) (	Do. d3	)	**16.** (		) (	Δ6	) (		)
12. (		) (	m6	) (		)	**17.** (		) (		) (	d6	)
13. (	A3	) (		) (		)	**18.** (Do. A2	) (		) (		)
14. (		) (	Δ7	) (		)	**19.** (		) (		) (	Do. d8	)

DRILL STUDY #4

Instructions: In Exercises 1–4, assume that each measure is incorrectly notated. Proceed by properly grouping each exercise and using numbers and brackets for each borrowed grouping encountered. More than one solution may be possible in some measures. After checking and correcting your work, it is highly recommended that you sing each corrected exercise individually or in an ensemble. Attempt to perform each exercise at the tempo indicated.

Instructions: In Exercises 5–8, provide the missing bar lines and correctly notate each measure within each exercise. Assume that all of the notation presented is incorrectly scored and that instances of borrowed division exist in each exercise. Use numbers and brackets for borrowed-division groupings. More than one solution may be possible in some measures. Perform these exercises individually or in groups, and set your own tempos.

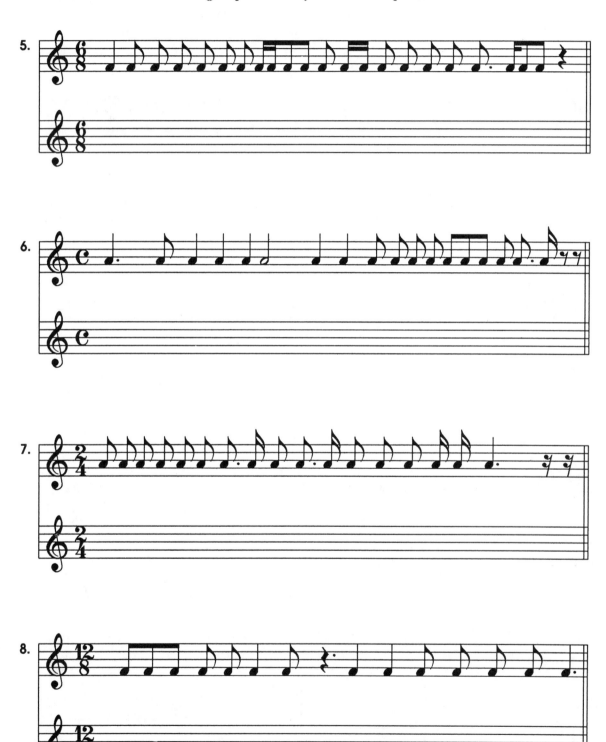

ASSIGNMENT FOR CHAPTER 8

NAME _____ SCORE _____ GRADE _____

DATE DUE _____ SECTION _____ INSTRUCTOR _____

1. *Instructions:* In each Part, (a)–(f), identify the mixture of diatonic and chromatic intervals.

(a)
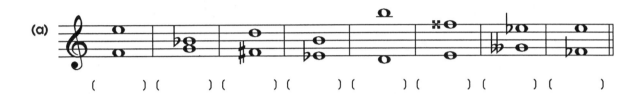
(   ) (   ) (   ) (   ) (   ) (   ) (   ) (   )

(b)
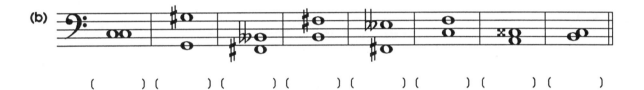
(   ) (   ) (   ) (   ) (   ) (   ) (   ) (   )

(c)
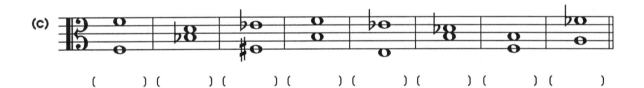
(   ) (   ) (   ) (   ) (   ) (   ) (   ) (   )

(d)
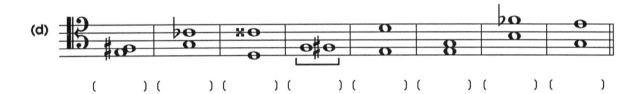
(   ) (   ) (   ) (   ) (   ) (   ) (   ) (   )

(e)
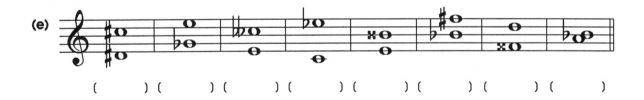
(   ) (   ) (   ) (   ) (   ) (   ) (   ) (   )

(f)

(   ) (   ) (   ) (   ) (   ) (   ) (   ) (   )

2. *Instructions:* Supply the missing upper note to the diatonic and chromatic intervals of Parts (a) and (b).

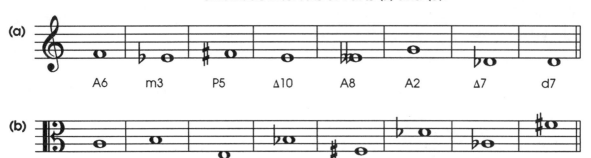

3. *Instructions:* Supply the missing lower note to the diatonic and chromatic intervals of Parts (a) and (b).

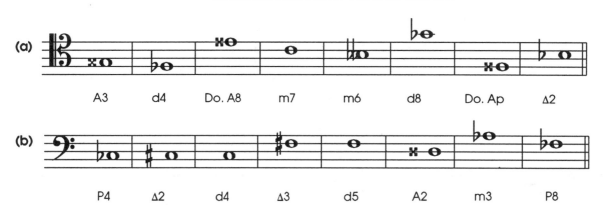

4. *Instructions:* Assume that the manuscripts in Parts (a) and (b) contain complete measures with some use of borrowed division, but that they are poorly written. Provide the proper beaming, bar lines, numbers, and brackets for all of the borrowed-division groupings. Place the solutions on the blank staff provided below each part. More than one solution may be possible for each part.

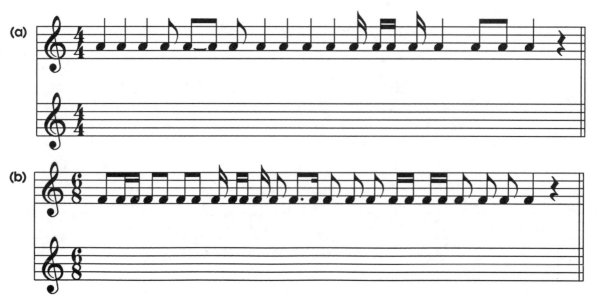

PERFORMANCE ASSIGNMENT FOT CHAPTER 8

Instructions: The material in this assignment is to be used for sight singing and ear training.

Suggested Mode of Practice

Both sets of drill exercises are meant to strengthen your understanding of borrowed division. Drills A and B, although written in different meters, sound exactly the same when performed in compound-duple and simple time, respectively. They are placed side by side in this study for the visual understanding and appreciation of this very complex rhythmic concept.

Study these two measure drills in the following manner:

1. Sing each exercise of Drill A in compound duple and each exercise of Drill B in simple time, making sure to give each note its full value.
2. Observe repeat signs.
3. Listen carefully to yourself for a more profound understanding of the material.
4. After each set of drill exercises, skip around and do each of them out of order to eliminate monotony and to heighten interest.
5. Broaden the rhythmic experience by changing tempos often.
6. After you have become familiar with the exercises, close your eyes and attempt to visualize the notation of each rhythmic exercise in your mind's eye as you perform them.

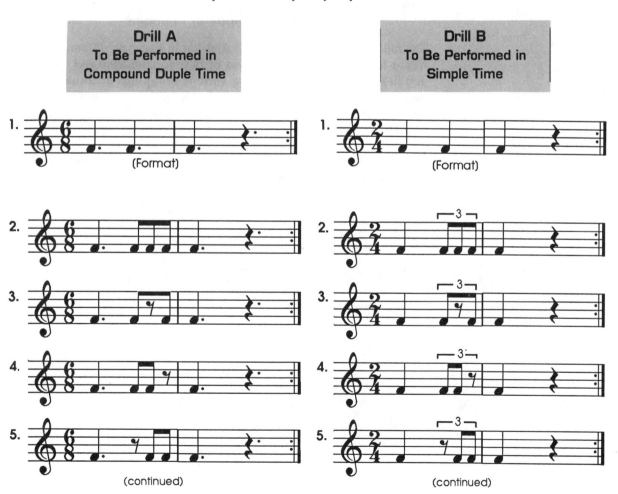

Drill A
To Be Performed in
Compound Duple Time

Drill B
To Be Performed in
Simple Time

(continued)

(continued)

Drill A (continued) **Drill B** (continued)

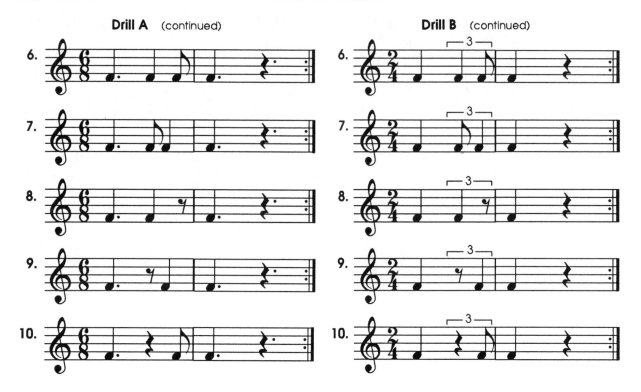

Duets of Borrowed Division

Suggested Mode of Practice

The following duets of borrowed division in Exercises 11 and 12 are meant to increase your awareness of beat subdivisions and to help you hear the effect of combining various groupings of sound. Sing each part of the duet individually to familiarize yourself with its contents and then perform it with a classmate as a duet. Listen carefully to each part as you participate. Each duet may be performed as a classroom drill. From a compositional point of view, the intended overuse of borrowed-division groupings in a three-bar phrase tends to be rather tedious; its use here is solely for learning purposes and the groupings are not intended as a model for music composition.

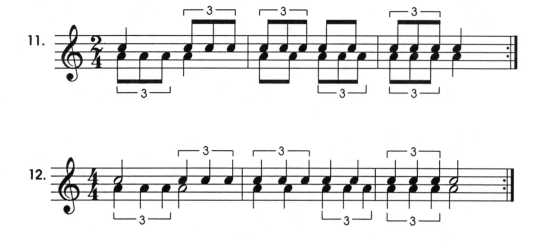

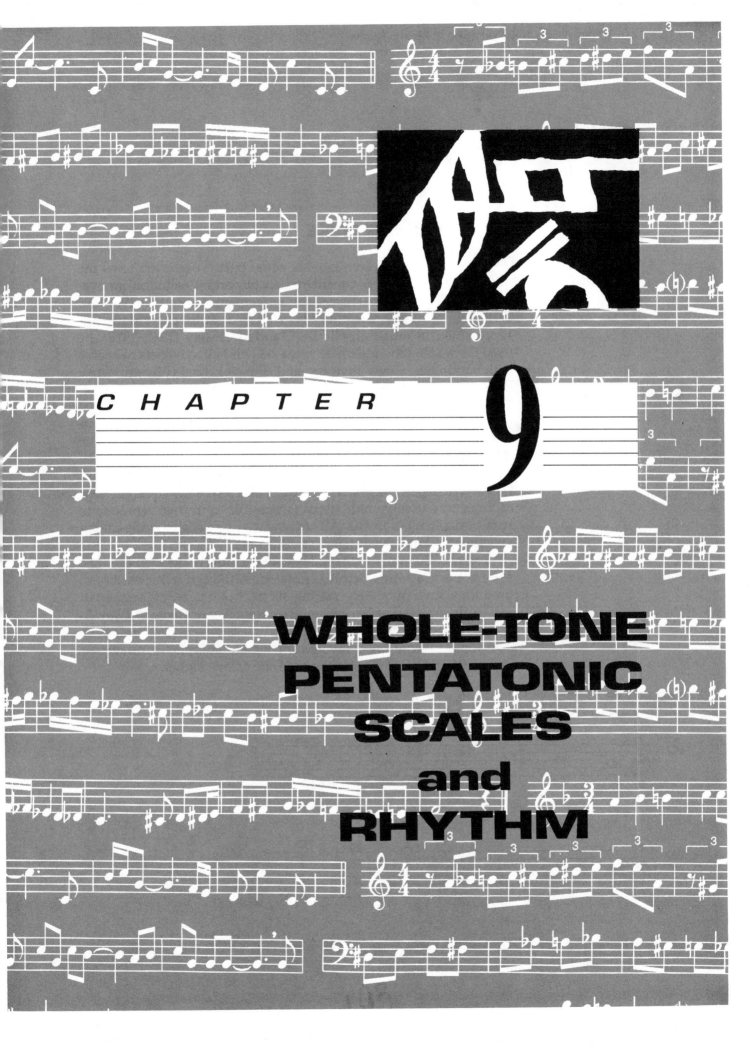

CHAPTER

9

WHOLE-TONE
PENTATONIC
SCALES
and
RHYTHM

Section

1

Pitch Considerations

THE WHOLE-TONE SCALE

The division of an octave into six equal parts is referred to as the **whole-tone** scale; it is considered an important technical innovation in music history. The artistic movement of the late 19th and early 20th centuries commonly referred to as **impressionism** was represented in music chiefly by Claude Debussy (1862–1918); he used the whole-tone scale with great skill and effectiveness to enable lush harmonies, subtle rhythms, and unusual tonal colors to evoke moods and impressions. Its use today by composers is sporadic; nevertheless, it is important to the student of theory.

The principal interval of the scale and the basis for its construction is the whole step. When set into a successive series of six whole steps, a scale is derived. In practice, a whole-tone scale may be found or placed upon any **degree** (whole step) of the keyboard; however, it should be understood that since a six-way equal division of an octave (twelve half steps) is possible, only two whole-tone scales exist in all of music. All other whole-tone scales represent the same pitches but with different starting notes.

Perhaps the most bothersome aspect of deriving a whole-tone scale is the way in which it is notated. Although it is possible to produce a scale by merely placing six pitches one whole step apart and in alphabetical order, it is not the acceptable or preferred way. In the following example, two versions of the same scale are presented; notational scheme (b) is favored for its less complex construction and its reiteration of the starting note one octave higher.

Example 98

Two versions of the whole-tone scale.

(a)

(b)

WRITING WHOLE-TONE SCALES

In writing whole-tone scales, the following pertinent points should be observed.

1. Begin by placing the desired clef and octave keynotes in position on the staff.

2. Starting with the upper keynote and working backwards, place a pitch on the staff that reflects a distance of a whole step. These two upper notes of the scale will involve a single letter change. Or, to put it another way, the interval between the lower keynote and the sixth scale degree will always outline an interval of a minor seventh.

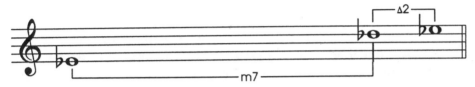

3. Fill in the remaining scale degrees, making sure that each pitch represents one whole step. Observe the interval of the essential diminished third within the scale. Without its presence, the reiteration of the octave keynote would not be possible. Incidentally, the placement of the diminished third may appear anywhere within a scale, with one exception; it should not be placed between the sixth and seventh degrees. The resulting scale in the example shown is a whole-tone scale written in E♭.

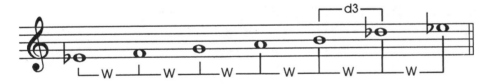

The following additional comments should prove helpful in the total understanding of this very unique scale. Key signatures that suggest tonality do not exist as a direct result of the whole-tone formula. With the scale equally divided and, consequently, with no single tone achieving any degree of prominence, no whole-tone scale by or of itself can convincingly express a feeling of tonality. However, composers can and have written whole-tone passages within tonally oriented compositions by merely supplying accidentals to the appropriate notes involved. Examine the following whole-tone scale written within the framework of A major.

Example 99

A whole-tone scale in A major.

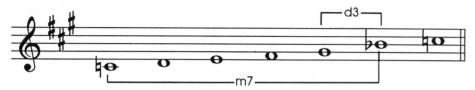

Notational characters, such as flats, sharps, double flats, double sharps, and even naturals, may be mixed in the notating of whole-tone scales. Since tonality is of no consequence, accidentals may be mixed freely.

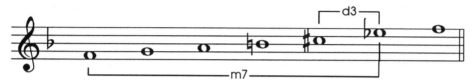

Finally, the method that has been prescribed for notating these scales is intended to serve the needs of the composer as well as those of the performer. If an occasion warrants a departure from what is recommended, then by all means, it should be employed. Thus, there is no correct or best method but, rather, a preferred or favored method. It should be understood that the system presented will satisfy the majority of situations and should lend a much needed hand towards consistency in manuscript notation.

Example 100

Variations in notating whole-tone scales.

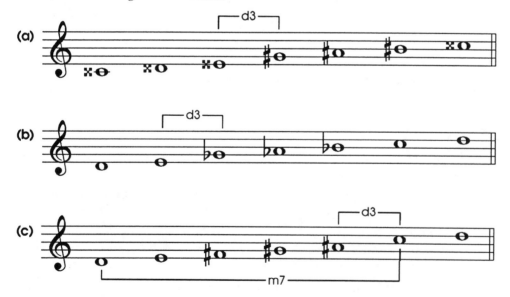

In Example 100, all three scales vary in their construction. In the first instance, scales (a) and (b) involve the unnecessary use of complicated accidentals (double sharps) and, in the second instance, they utilize flats ascending, which is, in general, contrary to what we have learned about scale construction. Both scales create enormous potential for possible reading problems during performance. Scale (c), however, conforms to the prescribed formula for writing whole-tone scales; in addition, it utilizes sharps ascending and is relatively easy to read. Each of these factors contribute to the overall acceptance of its notation by musicians and, indeed, this is the preferred and favored version.

THE PENTATONIC SCALE

The chief use of **pentatonic scales** is found in the area of melodic invention. They are scales whose five tones create the melodic basis for many popular songs, spirituals, folk songs, country-and-western type melodies, symphonic themes, and jazz compositions. Pentatonic scales occur in many early music cultures, in China, Africa, and the islands of the Pacific, as well as among Europeans and Native Americans. In the area of jazz improvisation, pentatonic scales, when combined with **blues notes** (flatted notes created by lowering various pitches one half step within the scale), may well form the basis for learning jazz improvisation.

For the most part, pentatonic scales are pleasing to the ear and are generally easy to sing. Their popularity, most assuredly, rests in the absence of any awkward or difficult intervals commonly found in other kinds of scales.

At this point, a closer look at the importance of a particularly dissonant and awkward interval found in diatonic major and minor scales should provide valuable insights into the construction of pentatonic scales. The interval in question, which consists of three whole tones, is referred to as the **tritone**.

THE TRITONE

Centuries ago, early musicians of the cloth called the *tritone* "*Diabolus in Musica*." This reference to the devil was based upon a concern for the awkwardness and dissonance found in the tritone interval of the augmented fourth or diminished fifth. However unacceptable this interval may have been, it was found to be extremely vital. Strategically placed and properly resolved within a traditional musical context, it provides the very essence of tonality—the establishment of a tonal key center.

A **tritone** can occur in three ways: first, it may appear within a composition as a **conjunct** (melodic motion by step) or **disjunct** (melodic motion by skip) melodic figure containing four tones and consisting of three whole steps whose outer limits outline the dissonant interval of an augmented fourth or diminished fifth.

Example 101

A tritone as a melody in conjunct motion and as a melody in disjunct motion.

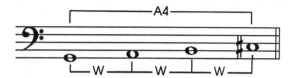

This melodic treatment of the tritone is referred to as a melody in conjunct motion. Its range or compass of sound is an augmented fourth.

This melodic treatment of the tritone is referred to as a melody in disjunct motion. Its range or compass of sound is a diminished fifth.

Secondly, it may not appear in either conjunct or disjunct form, but simply as either an interval of an augmented fourth or inverted as an interval of a diminished fifth, melodically or harmonically. In either case, augmented or diminished, the same characteristics are shared.

Example 102

A tritone as an interval of an augmented fourth and a tritone as an interval of a diminished fifth.

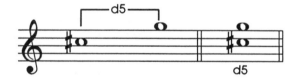

Thirdly, it may appear within a tonal context of a major or minor (harmonic or melodic form) key scheme. When found in this manner, it is referred to as the **tonal tritone**. This very important and necessary interval is represented by the combination of the fourth and seventh degrees of the scale; moreover, it is the specific combination and placement of tones that provide the melodic as well as harmonic impetus for tonal resolution. This gravitational pull provides the necessary tonal flavor for what is referred to as **tonality**, the tonal center, or key. The resolution of the tonal tritone is aimed at the tonic (1) and mediant (3) degrees of the major or minor scale, thus suggesting that traditionally augmented intervals resolve outwardly, while diminished intervals resolve inwardly.

Example 103

Resolution of the tonal tritone.

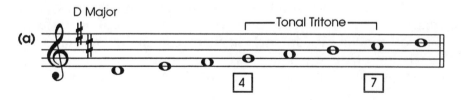

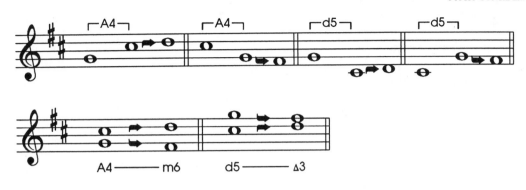

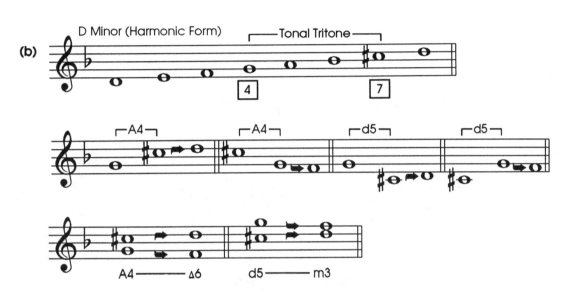

WRITING PENTATONIC SCALES

Pentatonic scales can be constructed upon all of the major and minor keynotes of our tonal system; therefore, it is both practical and possible to have fifteen major and fifteen minor pentatonic scales. Although some music theorists question the existence or validity of the minor pentatonic scale, further discussion of this matter is of little consequence and is not within the purview of this book. The position held by this author is that elements of minor pentatonic scales are heard routinely and extensively. Diverse music cultures use them, and even rock and jazz musicians employ them in their improvisations. For the aforementioned reasons, the inclusion of studies involving the minor pentatonic scale is a necessity for a thorough understanding of music theory.

The notating of major and minor pentatonic scales is simply a matter of selecting the proper key signature and removing certain tritones found in the major and minor key schemes. In the major pentatonic scale the tonal tritone is removed. In the minor pentatonic scale the interval of the diminished fifth found between the second and sixth degrees of the natural minor scale is removed. As in our previous study of scales, each is written within the architectural limits of one octave.

Example 104

The notation of major and minor pentatonic scales.

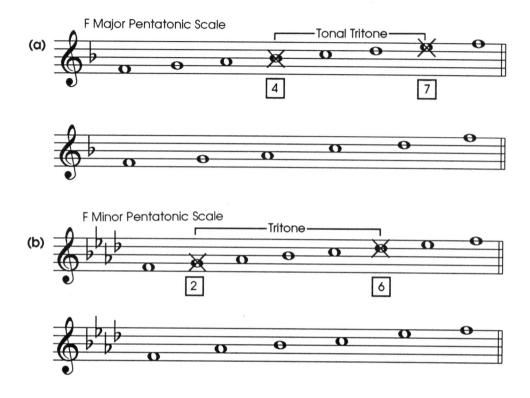

INSTANT MODAL TRANSPOSITION

The act of quickly determining which key signature should apply to a transposed mode is a valuable asset to the improvisor/performer or arranger/composer. The following method, referred to as **instant modal transposition**, provides this most important and valuable time-saving device.

The method is based upon the relationship of scale degrees within the Ionian mode, a scale-degree alignment in which the Dorian, Phrygian, Lydian, Mixolydian, Aeolian, and Locrian modes are always located on the 2nd, 3rd, 4th, 5th, 6th, and 7th degrees, respectively. Furthermore, this scale-degree alignment and the relationship to its Ionian will produce the means for determining each key signature, instantaneously. Memorize the interval relationship between the Ionian mode and its modal degrees.

Example 105

The Ionian mode and its modal degrees.

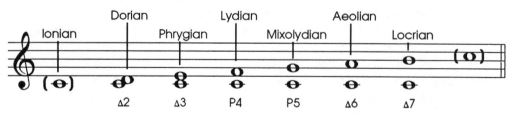

To define more clearly the method for obtaining key signatures for transposed modes instantaneously, study the solutions that follow. Note the mental process involved in each solution and be able to apply the interval relationship to each transposed mode.

Solution No. 1

Question:

Which key signature would apply to a G Dorian mode?

Mental Process:

Since the distance from the scale position of a Dorian mode to that of its related Ionian mode is a major second, the key signature of a G Dorian mode will always be found a major second, or one whole step, lower than its keynote. In other words, the key signature of a transposed mode will always be the same as its related Ionian mode.

Answer:

The key signature of a G Dorian mode will be that of the key of F major.

Solution No. 2

Question:

Which key signature would apply to an E Mixolydian mode?

Mental Process:

The distance from the keynote of a Mixolydian mode to that of its related Ionian mode is a perfect fifth. Thus, A is a perfect fifth below E.

Answer:

The key signature of an E Mixolydian mode will be that of the key of A major.

As a final summation of the scale-degree alignment and interval relationships among modes within a tonality, carefully examine the following material. Note that each related mode, although using different starting keynotes and randomly chosen octaves, will still use the key signature of D major.

Example 106

The related modes of the scale of D major.

Related Modes	Scale Displacement	Interval Relationship
Ionian	$d^1 - d^2$	
Dorian	$e^2 - e^3$	Down a Δ2
Phrygian	$f\#^1 - f\#^2$	Down a Δ3
Lydian	$g^2 - g^3$	Down a P4
Mixolydian	$a^3 - a^4$	Down a P5
Aeolian	$b^2 - b^3$	Down a Δ6
Locrian	$c\#^1 - c\#^2$	Down a Δ7

Example 107 contains four different modes chosen at random. Each scale displacement, interval relationship, and key-signature solution is presented for study.

Example 107

Four individual modal transpositions.

Transposed Mode	Scale Displacement	Interval Relationship	Key Signature to be Utilized
B♭ Dorian	$b\flat - b\flat^1$	Down a Δ2	A♭ major
A♭ Mixolydian	$a\flat^1 - a\flat^2$	Down a P5	D♭ major
D Phrygian	$d^1 - d^2$	Down a Δ3	B♭ major
C♯ Aeolian	$c\# - c\#^1$	Down a Δ6	E major

Section

2

The Notation of Rhythm

ANACRUSIS

Very often, a melodic line will start with what is referred as an *anacrusis*. An **anacrusis** is an unstressed pickup or lead-in note or group of notes that precedes the first accented note of a **phrase** (a short unit of musical line). The accented note of the phrase is found in the first complete measure of music. The anacrusis or pickup measure that precedes the first complete measure is not referred to as the first measure of the composition. In order for a measure to qualify as a complete measure, a full number of beats should be present, regardless of how the composition begins.

Example 108

An anacrusis.

MANUSCRIPT TIPS

The notating of an anacrusis in manuscript demands additional information and attention. As shown in Example 108, the anacrusis lacks a sufficient number of beats to qualify as a complete measure. Traditionally, in a completed composition, every attempt is made to have a sufficient number of beats in each measure according to the metric design of the work. That is to say, a full number of beats should be present, regardless of how the piece begins. If the anacrusis is attached to a section that is to be repeated, then the ending measure of that phrase should contain the missing beats of the anacrusis measure. If, however, the anacrusis is attached to a composition that does not repeat the anacrusis phrase or section, then the score should reflect a complete final measure. Study the contrasting illustrations in Example 109 and note the differences. Measure numbers are provided.

Example 109

Contrasting illustrations of the anacrusis.

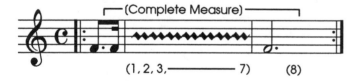

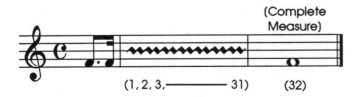

Manuscript Practice

Use these manuscript pages for note taking and drill.

DRILL STUDY #1

Instructions: On the staffs provided in Exercises 1–6, write the designated ascending or descending whole-tone scales. The bracket below each staff indicates the placement of the minor seventh interval.

1. D♭ Whole Tone (Ascending)

—m7—

2. F♯ Whole Tone (Descending)

—m7—

3. C♯ Whole Tone (Ascending)

—m7—

4. G Whole Tone (Descending)

—m7—

5. A♭ Whole Tone (Ascending)

—m7—

6. B Whole Tone (Descending)

—m7—

Instructions: On the staffs provided in Exercises 7–12, write the designated ascending or descending whole-tone scale within the tonal framework of each given key signature. Refer to the chapter as often as is necessary and reexamine the use of accidentals.

7. C Whole Tone (Ascending)

8. E♭ Whole Tone (Descending)

9. E Whole Tone (Ascending)

10. F♯ Whole Tone (Descending)

11. D Whole Tone (Ascending)

12. A Whole Tone (Descending)

DRILL STUDY #2

Instructions: As in Exercise 1, complete the sentences in Exercises 2–20 by naming the tonal tritone for each major and minor tonality in the blanks provided. Be sure to use the harmonic or melodic form of the underlined minor tonalities to obtain the tonal tritone.

1. The tonal tritone of the key of G♭ major is ___c♭___ and ___f___ .

2. The tonal tritone of the key of D major is _____ and _____ .

3. The tonal tritone of the key of B♭ minor is _____ and _____ .

4. The tonal tritone of the key of C minor is _____ and _____ .

5. The tonal tritone of the key of C major is _____ and _____ .

6. The tonal tritone of the key of F minor is _____ and _____ .

7. The tonal tritone of the key of B major is _____ and _____ .

8. The tonal tritone of the key of D minor is _____ and _____ .

9. The tonal tritone of the key of E major is _____ and _____ .

10. The tonal tritone of the key of F major is _____ and _____ .

11. The tonal tritone of the key of C♯ minor is _____ and _____ .

12. The tonal tritone of the key of G major is _____ and _____ .

13. The tonal tritone of the key of B minor is _____ and _____ .

14. The tonal tritone of the key of A♭ major is _____ and _____ .

15. The tonal tritone of the key of E♭ major is _____ and _____ .

16. The tonal tritone of the key of A♯ minor is _____ and _____ .

17. The tonal tritone of the key of G♯ minor is _____ and _____ .

18. The tonal tritone of the key of B♭ major is _____ and _____ .

19. The tonal tritone of the key of D♯ minor is _____ and _____ .

20. The tonal tritone of the key of A♭ minor is _____ and _____ .

Instructions: On the staffs provided in Exercises 21–26, write the designated ascending or descending major pentatonic scales. Be sure to use the appropriate key signature for each scale utilizing only six pitches.

21. C Major Pentatonic (Ascending)

22. D Major Pentatonic (Descending)

23. G Major Pentatonic (Ascending)

24. E Major Pentatonic (Descending)

25. B♭ Major Pentatonic (Ascending)

26. A♭ Major Pentatonic (Descending)

DRILL STUDY #3

Instructions: On the staffs provided in Exercises 1–6, write the designated ascending or descending minor pentatonic scales. Be sure to use the appropriate key signature for each scale, utilizing only six pitches.

1. C Minor Pentatonic (Ascending)

2. B♭ Minor Pentatonic (Descending)

3. F♯ Minor Pentatonic (Ascending)

4. C♯ Minor Pentatonic (Descending)

5. A♭ Minor Pentatonic (Ascending)

6. B Minor Pentatonic (Descending)

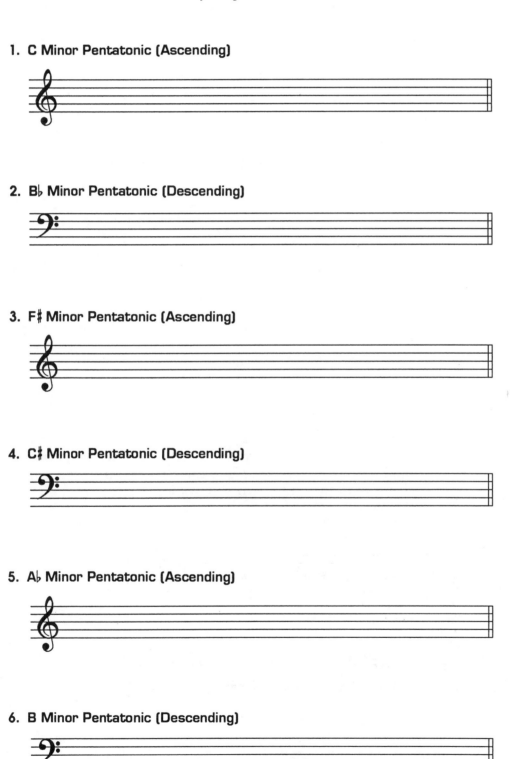

7. *Instructions:* The following drill is patterned after the explanation on instant modal transposition. As in Part (a), fill in the missing unknown and refer to the chapter as often as is necessary.

	Transposed Mode	Scale Displacement	Interval Relationship	Key Signature to be Used
(a)	D Dorian	_d1_ – _d2_	Down a _△2_	_C_ major
(b)	C Phrygian	____ – ____	Down a ____	____ major
(c)	D Lydian	____ – ____	Down a ____	____ major
(d)	B♭ Aeolian	____ – ____	Down a ____	____ major
(e)	B Mixolydian	____ – ____	Down a ____	____ major
(f)	C♯ Dorian	____ – ____	Down a ____	____ major
(g)	D Locrian	____ – ____	Down a ____	____ major
(h)	F Phrygian	____ – ____	Down a ____	____ major
(i)	F♯ Mixolydian	____ – ____	Down a ____	____ major
(j)	A Aeolian	____ – ____	Down a ____	____ major

8. *Instructions:* Each individual line, (a)–(c), contains an anacrusis, and each rhythmic grouping within each line is written correctly. Supply the necessary bar lines to each individual rhythmic line, according to the designated meter. More than one solution is possible.

(a)

(b)

(c)

ASSIGNMENT FOR CHAPTER 9

NAME _____ SCORE _____ GRADE _____

DATE DUE _____ SECTION _____ INSTRUCTOR _____

1. *Instructions:* On the staffs provided, write the designated ascending or descending whole-tone scales. You may choose to incorporate the use of key signatures. Good manuscript is of paramount importance.

(a) B Whole Tone (Ascending)

(b) D♭ Whole Tone (Descending)

(c) F♯ Whole Tone (Ascending)

2. *Instructions:* On the staffs provided in parts (a)–(c), write the designated ascending or descending pentatonic scales. As in Exercise 1, you may choose to use key signatures.

(a) F♯ Major Pentatonic (Ascending)

(b) B Major Pentatonic (Descending)

(c) E♭ Minor Pentatonic (Ascending)

Instructions: In Exercises 3–12, fill in the missing unknowns relating to instant modal transposition.

Transposed Mode	Scale Displacement	Interval Relationship	Key Signature to be Used
3. E Aeolian	_____ – _____	Down a _____	_____ major
4. F♯ Dorian	_____ – _____	Down a _____	_____ major
5. C♯ Phrygian	_____ – _____	Down a _____	_____ major
6. G Mixolydian	_____ – _____	Down a _____	_____ major
7. F Locrian	_____ – _____	Down a _____	_____ major
8. A♭ Dorian	_____ – _____	Down a _____	_____ major
9. F Lydian	_____ – _____	Down a _____	_____ major
10. C Mixolydian	_____ – _____	Down a _____	_____ major
11. E♭ Dorian	_____ – _____	Down a _____	_____ major
12. G♯ Phrygian	_____ – _____	Down a _____	_____ major

13. *Instructions:* In Parts (a)–(c), each individual line contains an anacrusis; all rhythmic groupings are correct. Supply the necessary bar lines according to the designated meter. More than one solution is possible.

(a)

(b)

(c)

PERFORMANCE ASSIGNMENT FOR CHAPTER 9

Instructions: The material in this assignment is to be used for sight singing and ear training.

Suggested Mode of Practice

This series of drills is meant to help strengthen your understanding of sixteenth notes and combined rest groupings.

1. Sing each exercise and give each note its full value.
2. Be sure to observe the repeat sign.
3. Listen to yourself carefully for a more profound understanding of the material.
4. After each set of drills, skip around and do the drills out of order to eliminate monotony and to heighten interest.
5. Broaden the rhythmic experience by changing tempos often.
6. After you have sung each exercise through several times, close your eyes and attempt to visualize the notation of each written expression.

The ability to concentrate thoroughly in detail when hearing these rhythmic groupings will pay huge dividends when attempting melodic and rhythmic dictation.

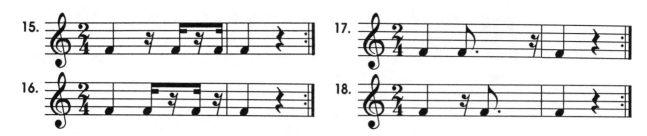

Instructions: Strive for excellence of performance with each musical segment presented in Exercises 19–24. Change tempos frequently and pay attention to detail.

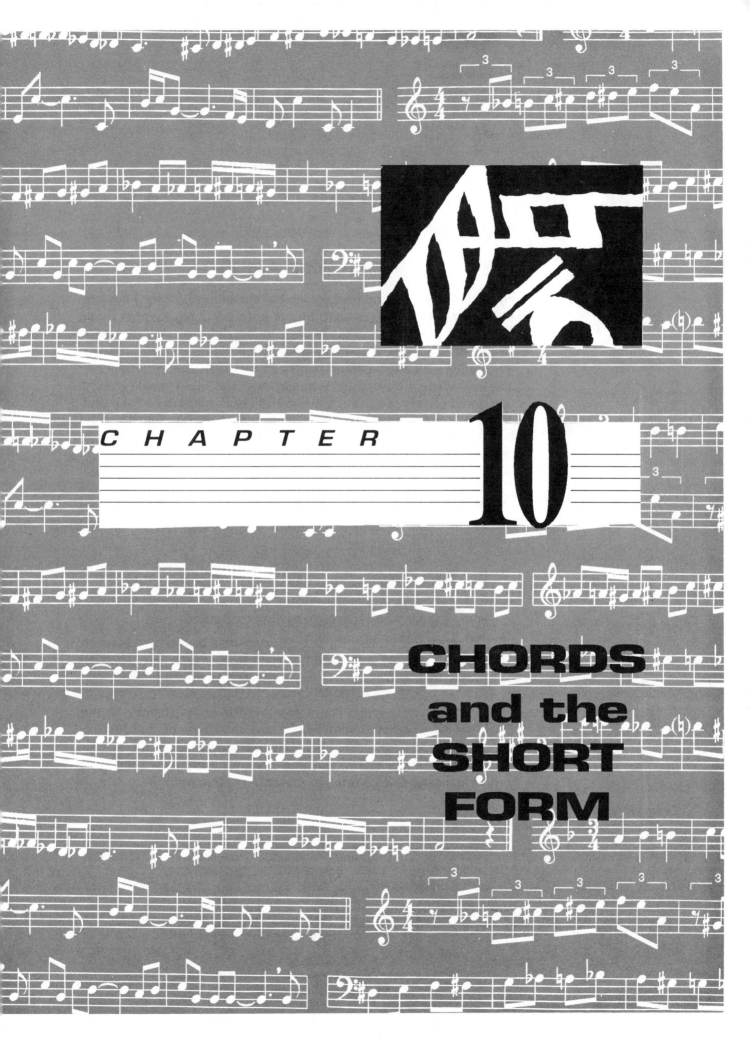

CHAPTER

10

**CHORDS
and the
SHORT
FORM**

Section

1

Pitch Considerations

THE ALPHABETICAL CHORD SYSTEM

Understanding the symbols found in the **alphabetical chord system,** in which the keynote or root tone of a chord is represented by an alphabetical letter name, has become an outright necessity for many musicians. Even the classroom teacher, who is called upon to interpret much of today's contemporary music, feels the importance of this knowledge. Newspapers, magazines, and other media publish lyrics and chords of current top hits and use this system. To the multitude of newly arrived guitarists, it is the only means of survival.

The chordal system employed is derived from diatonic major and minor scales. It is similar to the system that is taught in traditional harmony, with the one exception involving the use of uppercase letters (A, B, C, D, E, F, and G), rather than Roman numerals (I, ii, iii, IV, V, vi, vii°) for the naming of each degree of the scale.

There exists within this system three categories of chordal combinations:

1. Category I combines the sounds of three notes to form a triad.

2. Category II involves the addition of a fourth sound to an existing triad, and is referred to as a seventh chord.

3. Category III involves the use of extensions beyond the seventh, and these extensions are referred to as ninth, eleventh, or thirteenth chords.

Since many chord symbols are possible for each category, in this book the recommended symbol of a particular type of chord within a category will be placed in boldface and indicated by the symbol ➤. Chords representing the three main categories, including individual extension chords, are presented in Example 110.

Example 110

The three categories of chordal combinations.

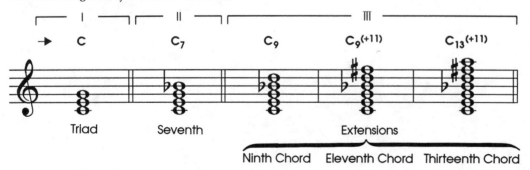

CATEGORY I – THE MAJOR TRIAD

A **triad** contains three tones:

1. a **root** tone, whose alphabetical letter name represents the triad;
2. a **third**, whose pitch lies the distance of a third above the root; and
3. a **fifth**, whose pitch lies the distance of a fifth above the root.

The triad is a **major triad** when the distance between the root and its third is major and the distance between the root and its fifth is perfect. Each major triad is specified by the single upper-case letter name of the root to indicate its major quality. At no time are there any additional indicators present, such as an abbreviation of major (maj.), or an upper-case M, or any other symbol.

Additionally, it should be understood that when the letter name of a chord involves a chromatic note, the chromatic sign is part of the chord symbol. That is to say, the letter name of the chord is exactly the same as the letter name of the root tone.

Example 111
Major triads.

CATEGORY I – THE MINOR TRIAD

A **minor triad** is one in which the distance between the root and its third is minor and the distance between the root and its fifth is perfect. Its symbol can be indicated in one of four possible ways, as illustrated in Example 112.

Example 112
Minor triads.

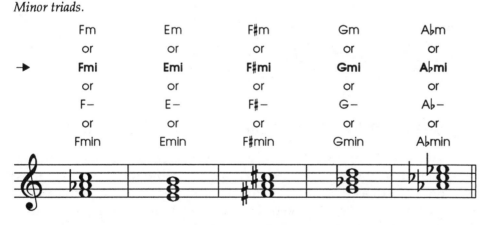

CATEGORY I – THE DIMINISHED TRIAD

The **diminished triad** contains a minor third and a diminished fifth above the root. A small circle (°) or the abbreviation "dim" is placed to the right of the letter name. A diminished triad can also be designated as a minor triad with a lowered fifth. Its symbol can be shown in one of four possible ways. Note carefully the interchangeability of the flat and the minus sign as well as of the sharp and the plus sign within the parentheses.

Example 113
Diminished triads.

Fdim	Edim	F♯dim	Gdim	G♯dim
or	or	or	or	or
Fmi⁽⁻⁵⁾	Emi⁽♭⁵⁾	F♯mi⁽⁻⁵⁾	Gmi⁽♭⁵⁾	G♯mi⁽⁻⁵⁾
or	or	or	or	or
F−⁽♭⁵⁾	E−⁽⁵⁾	F♯−⁽♭⁵⁾	G−⁽⁵⁾	G♯−⁽♭⁵⁾
or	or	or	or	or
F°	E°	F♯°	G°	G♯°

CATEGORY I – THE AUGMENTED TRIAD

The **augmented triad** contains a major third and an augmented fifth above the root. The augmented fifth interval may be shown in a number of ways: by a plus five (+5) or a sharp five (♯5) in parentheses, by a plus sign, +, without parentheses, or simply, by the abbreviation "aug." In all cases, each symbol, when placed to the right of the chord letter name, designates the same thing.

Example 114
Augmented triads.

F⁺	E⁺	F♯⁺	G⁺	A♭⁺
or	or	or	or	or
F⁽⁺⁵⁾	E⁽♯⁵⁾	F♯⁽⁺⁵⁾	G⁽♯⁵⁾	A♭⁽⁺⁵⁾
or	or	or	or	or
Faug	Eaug	F♯aug	Gaug	A♭aug

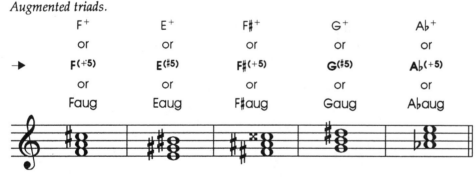

CATEGORY I – THE DOMINANT-RELATED TRIADS

Two additional triads for study are considered primarily "dominant-related." Although they often appear in triadic form, they are most often heard as part of the second-chord category and specifically, as part of the dominant seventh chord. They are presented at this time because of their unique triadic construction.

The lowered fifth, (−5) or (♭5), placed to the right of any uppercase letter name and enclosed in parentheses, makes reference to a triad with a major third and a diminished fifth above the root. This **dominant-related triad** with the lowered fifth can be indicated in two possible ways. *Both* are recommended.

Example 115

Altered dominant triads.

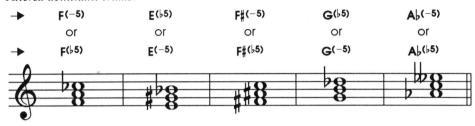

The second dominant-related triad contains a perfect fourth and a perfect fifth. What makes this "sus four" (suspended fourth) so unique is its discarded third. Note that the symbol may be indicated in four possible ways. The first one is recommended.

Example 116

Sus four chords.

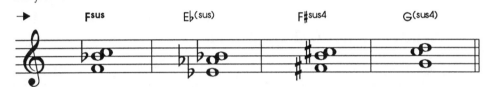

By way of review, there are essentially two kinds of triads: major and minor. Four types are found in the major group:

1. a triad with a major third and a perfect fifth (*major triad*),

2. a triad with a major third and an augmented fifth (*augmented triad*),

3. a special triad having a major third and a diminished fifth (*dominant-related with a lowered fifth*), and

4. another special triad having a perfect fourth and a perfect fifth (*dominant-related "sus four"*).

In the minor group, two types exist:

1. a triad with a minor third and a perfect fifth (*minor triad*) and

2. a triad with a minor third and a diminished fifth (*diminished triad*).

Now review each group and triad presented in this chapter individually. In addition, memorize the interval schematic and the recommended symbol for each type of triad.

CATEGORY II – THE INTERVAL OF THE SEVENTH

Three qualities of minor seventh intervals are used in combination with various triads to form seventh chords. These intervals of the seventh are

1. the major seventh,

2. the minor seventh, and

3. the diminished seventh.

It is important to note that two of these intervals, when combined with particular triads, are represented differently in chord symbols than in interval identification. For instance, the minor seventh interval does *not* use any modifiers, but is simply represented by an Arabic number seven (7), and the diminished seventh interval is represented by a small raised circle, which is placed between the letter name of the chord and the number seven in the following manner:

$$X°7$$

Example 117
Intervals of the seventh.

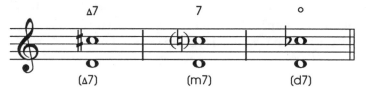

CATEGORY II – THE DOMINANT SEVENTH CHORD

As we have previously seen, the fifth degree of the diatonic major or minor scale is referred to as the dominant; moreover, when one places a major triad on this degree, it is referred to as the **dominant triad**. If an interval of a minor seventh is added to this existing dominant triad, a category-two chord is created: namely the dominant seventh chord.

Although intervals of the seventh can be added to other triads located on the various degrees of the major or minor scale, only one dominant seventh chord exists per tonality. The combination of a major triad and a minor seventh interval forms this very unique seventh chord.

Study the two-part Example 118, for it more graphically describes what has been presented.

Example 118
Locating and defining the dominant seventh chord.

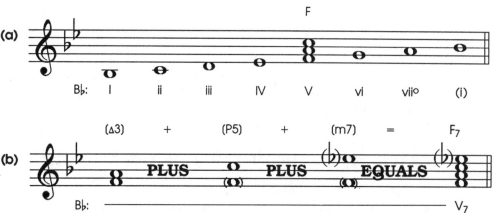

CATEGORY II – THE ALTERED AND "SUS FOUR" DOMINANTS

Three more dominant seventh chords remain to be presented. Two of them have already been partially introduced with the discussion on dominant-related triads. The third and final dominant seventh chord to be presented involves the combining of an augmented triad and a minor seventh interval. The combination of a lowered or raised fifth on a dominant seventh chord is commonly referred to as an **altered dominant**.

The word "sus" is an abbreviation for **suspension**, which was a concept commonly found in compositions of the baroque period (1600–1750). This concept made reference to placing a nonharmonic tone on a rhythmically strong beat in place of a normally expected chord tone. Suspensions have been part of music literature for over three centuries and continue to be used in all facets of music composition.

Finally, compare those dominants whose fifths are altered and memorize their recommended symbols. In addition, attempt to visualize the unique construction of the **dominant seventh "sus four" chord**, a dominant seventh in which an interval of a perfect fourth is substituted for the interval of the discarded third. This construction is shown in Example 119.

Example 119

The various dominant seventh chords.

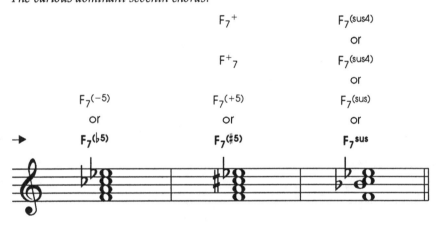

CATEGORY II – THE MINOR SEVENTH CHORDS

This group of the **minor seventh chords** combines the minor triad and the interval of the minor seventh. It is important to remember that the minor seventh interval is represented by the number seven, and that the abbreviation "mi" in the chord symbol makes reference to the minor triad.

Example 120

The minor seventh chord.

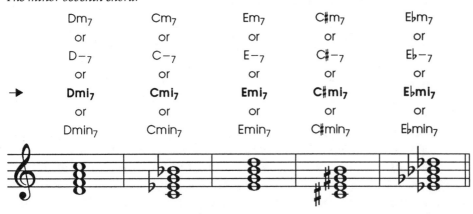

CATEGORY II – THE HALF-DIMINISHED SEVENTH CHORD

The **half-diminished seventh chord** is also known as the **minor seventh chord with a flatted fifth**. It is different from the previously introduced minor seventh chord by virtue of its diminished triad. Because of this construction, it can be referred to as a *minor seventh with a flatted fifth* or, simply, as a *half-diminished seventh* chord. A small raised circle with a slash through it ($^{\varnothing}$) is used as one of the recommended ways of denoting the half-diminished seventh chord.

Example 121

The half-diminished seventh chord.

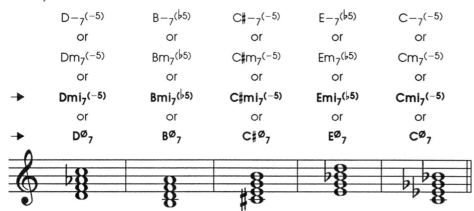

CATEGORY II – THE FULLY DIMINISHED SEVENTH CHORD

The *fully diminished seventh* chord is closely related to the half-diminished seventh chord; as diminished chords, they share a similar construction. They both contain diminished triads; however, the similarity ends with the interval of the seventh. The **fully diminished seventh chord** employs a diminished seventh, instead of a minor seventh interval.

The notating of fully diminished seventh chords deserves some attention. As a chord type, fully diminished seventh chords employ *options*. These options allow the interchanging of sharps and flats within an alignment and, in some cases, involve enharmonic spellings. For example, the diminished seventh interval is often notated as a major sixth. Enharmonic equivalents are recommended in place of double flats as well as in place of the two troublesome pitches of "f flat" and "c flat." If possible, flatted root tones are also to be avoided; however, there are times, harmonically, when a sharped root, originally chosen as an option for a flatted root, may conflict with the intention of the progression and, as such, is best left alone. The choice between the major sixth and the diminished seventh interval, and/or the use of enharmonics is generally done, primarily, for ease of reading. Each of the aforementioned choices of optional notation is correct and entirely acceptable and is furthermore lauded by the performing musician.

In Example 122, all types of fully diminished seventh chords are presented. Where the interchanging of the root has taken place, or where an interval preference is made, or in case enharmonic options are taken, all alignments are given. Study each type very carefully.

Example 122
Fully diminished seventh chords.

CATEGORY II – THE MAJOR SEVENTH CHORD

The **major seventh chord** contains a major triad and an interval of a major seventh. It can also use an interval of a major sixth as a seventh substitute and is then known as an **"add 6" chord**. This concept is not to be confused with the discussion of optional notation in the study of fully diminished seventh chords. Also, the major designation or modifier found in the symbol refers to the interval of the major seventh and *not* to the triad.

Example 123

The major seventh chord.

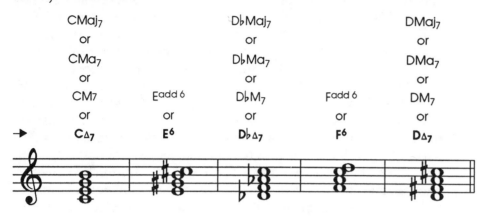

CATEGORY II – THE MINOR/MAJOR SEVENTH CHORD

The **minor/major seventh chord** is one of the most unique-sounding chords in the entire chordal system. It contains a minor triad and an interval of a major seventh. Having some of the same characteristics as the equivalent major chord, it, too, uses the interval of a major sixth in place of a major seventh interval as a seventh substitute.

Example 124

The minor/major seventh chord.

CHORDAL DERIVATION

Major and minor scales serve as the basis for all chord types and their particular harmonic functions. They provide the scale degrees upon which qualities of chord types are constructed and they serve as an important mode of entry into the study of chordal progressions. Although the study of traditional harmonic practice is not within the scope of this book, it is important to see the relationship between scale degrees and the derivation of chordal types. The following example of seventh chords provides scale-degree identification, chordal symbols, and the location of chordal qualities in a major-key scheme.

Example 125

Chordal types within a major tonality.

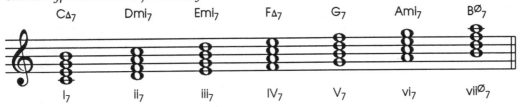

I_7 and IV_7 Chords = Major seventh chords

ii_7, iii_7, and vi_7 = Minor seventh chords

V_7 = Dominant seventh chord

$vii^\emptyset_7$ = Half-diminished seventh chord

Because three active scale forms exist in the minor tonality, a composite minor-scale example is necessary. Chordal derivation, scale-degree identification, chordal symbols, and chordal locations are identified and labeled according to minor-scale forms:

[N] = Natural,   [H] = Harmonic,   [M] = Melodic

Example 126

Chordal types within a minor composite.

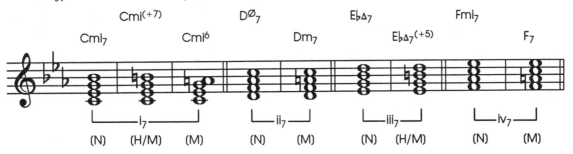

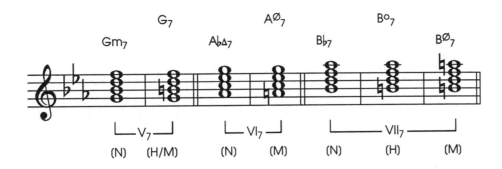

$i^{(+7)}$ = Minor/major seventh chord

i^6 = Minor add 6 chord

i_7, ii_7, iv_7, and v_7 = Minor seventh chords

$ii^\emptyset_7$, $vi^\emptyset_7$, and $vii^\emptyset_7$ = Half-diminished seventh chords

III_7 and VI_7 = Major seventh chords

III^+_7 = Major seventh chord with a raised fifth

IV_7, V_7, and VII_7 = Dominant seventh chords

vii^o_7 = Fully diminished seventh chord

CHORDAL EPILOGUE

The study of triads and seventh chords is a fundamental necessity for the musician. As stated before, it provides the entry and the basis for advanced study of more complex and profound concepts in music theory: *counterpoint*, *harmony*, and *composition*. For the jazz improvisor, it is an absolute necessity. The ability to analyze, play, and hear chordal alignments in their melodic and harmonic forms is paramount. Although the study of Category III chords is beyond the scope of this book, the fundamentals provided here on triads and sevenths chords should serve as a very strong foundation and, indeed, as the basis for a definitive study of extensions.

The student who reviews, practices, and uses the foundational studies of this chapter will continually gain technical facility and will, most certainly, enhance his or her knowledge of triadic and seventh-chord construction.*

Section

2

The Short Form

Generally, form is the organizational scheme that determines the basic structure of a musical composition. It involves all of the elements of music, including one of the most important aspects, the use of repetition. The repetition of sections or larger segments helps specify and detail the various boundaries of musical form. In this book, the phrase "**the short form**" is used to define a particular manner of performance, and although connected with form in the larger sense, it is not specific in terms of actual forms used in music, such as concertos, symphonies, sonatas, and so on.

---

*Another book written by this author, entitled, *All About Chords*, is more definitive in scope and is designed to follow this book. It deals with the practical application of *extensions*, *analysis*, and *chordal progressions*, and includes comprehensive exercise materials.

BINARY AND TERNARY FORMS

The analysis of musical form is governed primarily by the separation of the whole into its many parts and the examination of the relationship of these parts to the whole and to one another. Within this whole meaningful process, standard forms for analysis are necessary. Two very basic analytical forms exist. They are commonly referred to as **binary** (two-part) **form** and **ternary** (three-part) **form**. These two standard forms will serve as the basis for understanding the following repetition devices as they relate to manner of performance.

THE *DA CAPO* FORM

The Italian term "*da capo*" is frequently used in place of other repeat marks for sections or larger segments of music. It literally means, "from the head." The English translation of this phrase is "from the beginning." Sometimes this term is represented in music by the simple abbreviation "D.C." The manner of performance involves repetition.

The procedure for correctly performing a D.C. is simply to go back to the beginning of the composition and repeat the section that contains the directional phrase or abbreviation. Often, the abbreviation D.C. is expanded to a phrase such as **D.C. *al fine***, or **D.C. *al segno*** (𝄋 or ⊕), or even to the more definitive phrase, **D.C. *al segno e poi la coda***. In Italian the first phrase "*al fine*" means "to the end," the second phrase "*al segno*" means "to the sign," whereas the third and most definitive phrase means, literally, "to the sign and then the coda." Study the following diagrams on how D.C.'s work.

Da Capo

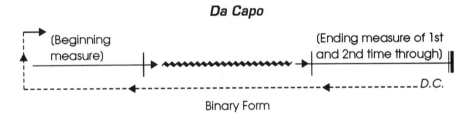

Binary Form

Da Capo al Fine

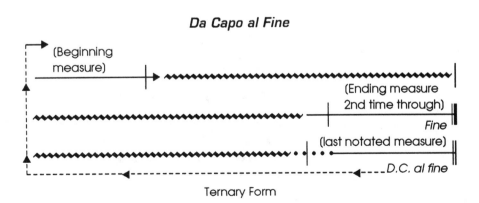

Ternary Form

Da Capo al Segno

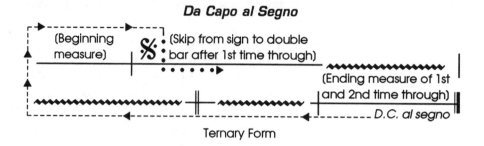

Ternary Form

Da Capo al Segno e poi la Coda

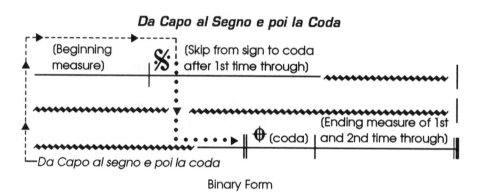

Binary Form

THE *DAL SEGNO* FORM

The single most important difference between *da capo* and *dal segno* centers around the question of where the repeat begins. Previously, in the discussion on *da capo*, all repeats began at the beginning of a composition. In the *dal segno* form, the repeat always begins at the point where the symbol (𝄋 or ✛) is placed.

Dal Segno

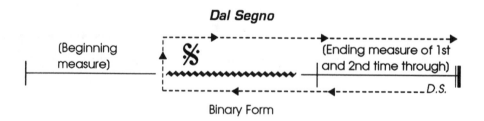

Binary Form

Dal Segno al Fine

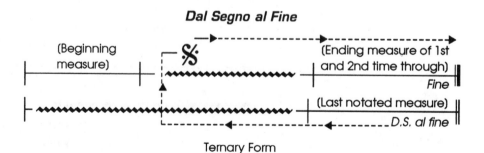

Ternary Form

FIRST AND SECOND ENDINGS

Although repetition yielded either binary or ternary forms in our previous discussion, *first and second endings* are, for the most part, binary; moreover, they tend to be much simpler in design and function than other forms of repetition.

The manner of performance involves the playing of an original section of music and taking what is referred to as the **first ending** and the repeat. During the repeat, the **second ending** is substituted for the first. It is simply a matter of "skipping" the first ending the second time through. Multiple endings of repeated sections are possible, but more than three endings are rarely seen in music literature.

First and Second Endings

MANUSCRIPT TIPS

The rules governing the alignment of chord tones and the placement of accidentals within a chordal structure are fairly consistent with what we know about interval alignment. By way of review, when starting with intervals of the second through the sixth, accidentals are placed closest to the upper note, whereas the lower accidental is placed diagonally to the left and is not aligned perpendicularly. Occasionally, when the upper note of the interval of the sixth is flatted, an accidental on the lower note may be aligned in a perpendicular fashion. Vertical intervals beyond a sixth and of larger dimension create no particular problems.

In a triadic structure in which three accidentals are required, the alignment process is as follows: if the top and bottom notes of the triad do not exceed the interval of a sixth, the highest accidental is placed first and closest to the uppermost note head, while the lowest accidental is placed second and diagonally to the left of the first. The middle, or central, accidental is placed last and farthest to the left. If the top and bottom notes are farther apart than a sixth, the highest and lowest accidentals are aligned vertically and the middle accidental is placed to the left. In chordal alignments in which three accidentals are required and an interval of a second is present, no special treatment is required, although some copyists treat the interval of the second first, and place the third accidental to the far left. Either method is acceptable.

Example 127

Alignment of accidentals in 3-part chordal structures.

The rules governing the placement of accidentals for seventh chords that contain four accidentals are usually very flexible; however, the rules governing triads still apply in most cases. That is, the highest and lowest accidentals are aligned whenever possible and the middle accidentals are arranged diagonally to the left from the highest to the lowest. A final word of caution concerning chordal alignment! Whenever the interval of the second is notated, it must always be written diagonally to the right and upward. Example 128 illustrates the common solutions to various placement problems with seventh chords containing multiple accidentals.

Example 128

Alignment of accidentals in 4-part chordal structures.

Manuscript Practice

Use these manuscript pages for note taking and drill.

DRILL STUDY #1

Instructions: In Exercises 1–3, identify the following triads. Place the answers above each triad on the lines provided, and try to use only the recommended symbols.

Instructions: In Exercises 4–6, supply the designated triads on the staffs provided. Various symbols are used to enhance your ability to recognize all chordal types instantly.

Instructions: In Exercises 7–9, identify the following triads. Place the answers on the lines provided above each triad, and try to use only the recommended symbols.

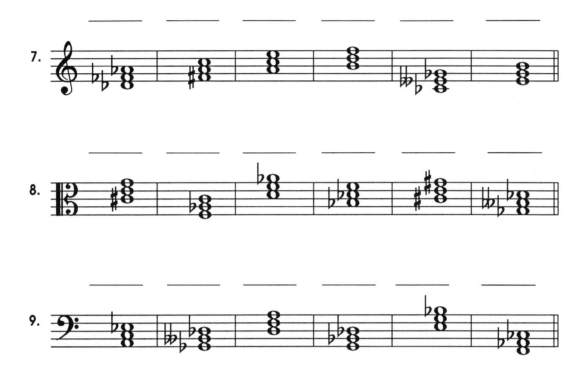

Instructions: In Exercises 10–12, supply the designated triads on the staffs provided. Various symbols are used to enhance your ability to recognize all chordal types instantly.

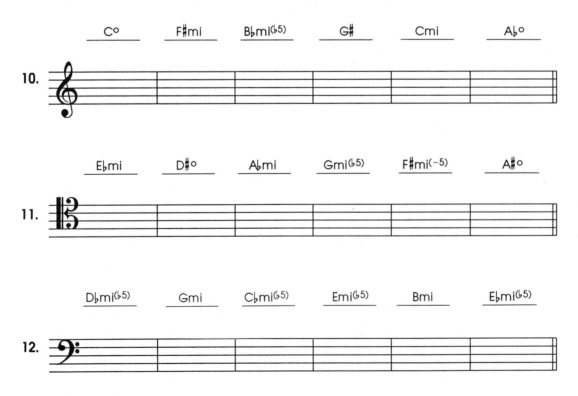

DRILL STUDY #2

Instructions: In Exercises 1–3, identify the following dominant seventh chords. Place the answers on the lines provided above each chord, and try to use only the recommended symbols.

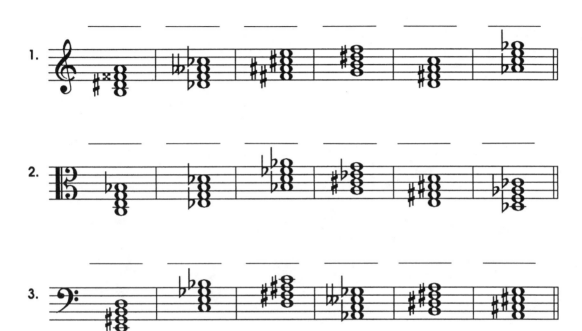

Instructions: In Exercises 4–6, supply the designated dominant seventh chords on the staffs provided. Various chordal symbols are used to enhance your ability to recognize this type of seventh chord instantly.

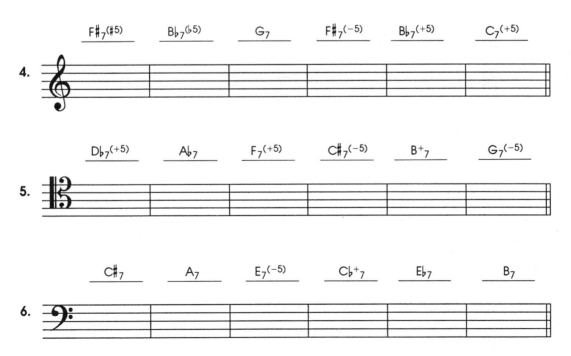

Instructions: In Exercises 7–9, identify each of the following seventh-chord qualities. Place the answers on the lines provided above each chord, and try to use only the recommended symbols.

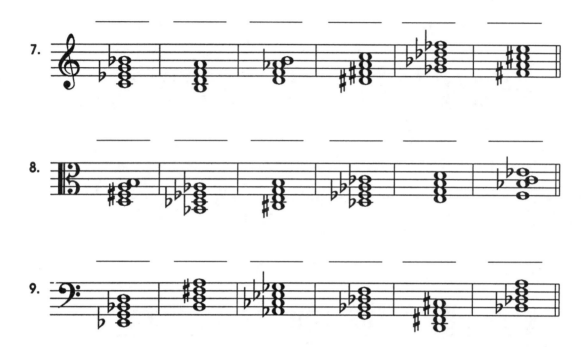

Instructions: In Exercises 10–12, supply the designated mixed-quality seventh chords on the staffs provided, taking all options regarding fully diminished seventh chords. Various chordal symbols are presented to enhance your ability to recognize quickly the various chord qualities found within the chordal system.

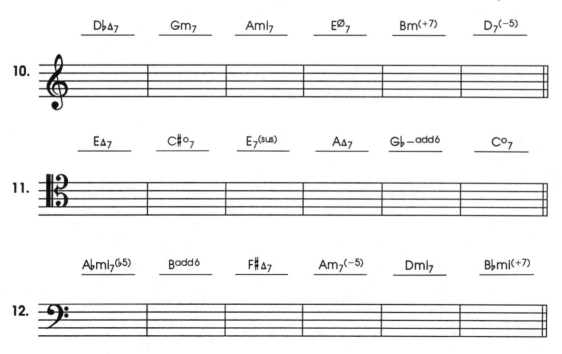

DRILL STUDY #3

Instructions: In Exercises 1–3, identify each of the following seventh-chord qualities. Place the answers on the lines provided above each chord, and try to use only recommended symbols.

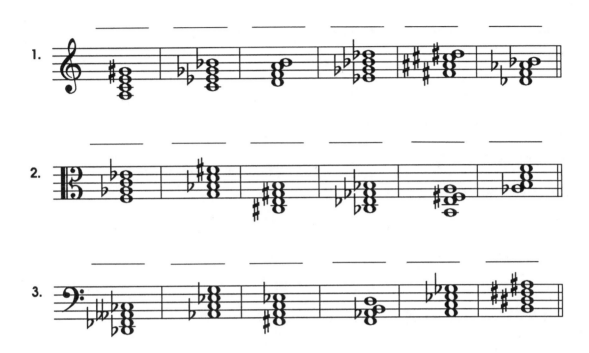

Instructions: In Exercises 4–6, supply the designated mixed-quality seventh chords on the staffs provided, taking all options regarding fully diminished seventh chords. Various chordal symbols are presented to enhance your ability to recognize quickly the various chord qualities found within the chordal system.

Instructions: As illustrated in Exercise 7, complete the statements concerning dominant seventh chords by filling in the blanks in Exercises 8–21.

7. The dominant seventh chord of G major is D_7 .

8. The dominant seventh chord of C♭ major is _____ .

9. The dominant seventh chord of F major is _____ .

10. The dominant seventh chord of G♭ major is _____ .

11. The dominant seventh chord of C major is _____ .

12. The dominant seventh chord of A♭ major is _____ .

13. The dominant seventh chord of D major is _____ .

14. The dominant seventh chord of F♯ minor (harmonic) is _____ .

15. The dominant seventh chord of E minor (harmonic) is _____ .

16. The dominant seventh chord of A♭ minor (harmonic) is _____ .

17. The dominant seventh chord of B minor (harmonic) is _____ .

18. The dominant seventh chord of C♯ minor (harmonic) is _____ .

19. The dominant seventh chord of G minor (harmonic) is _____ .

20. The dominant seventh chord of A minor (harmonic) is _____ .

21. The dominant seventh chord of G♯ minor (harmonic) is _____ .

Instructions: Exercises 22–26 are meant to monitor your understanding of the various "short forms" presented in this chapter. Use your own words to describe the manner of performance or definition for each expression given. Use the space provided after each question.

22. How does a binary form differ from a ternary form?

23. What is the chief difference between a performance of a *da capo* and a *dal segno* section in a composition?

24. Describe the manner of performance for a first and second ending.

25. Describe the manner of performance involving a *da capo al fine* section.

26. Describe the manner of performance involving a *dal segno al fine* section.

ASSIGNMENT FOR CHAPTER 10

NAME _____ SCORE _____ GRADE _____

DATE DUE _____ SECTION _____ INSTRUCTOR _____

1. *Instructions:* Identify each of the following triad and seventh-chord qualities. Place the answers above each chord, and use only recommended chord symbols.

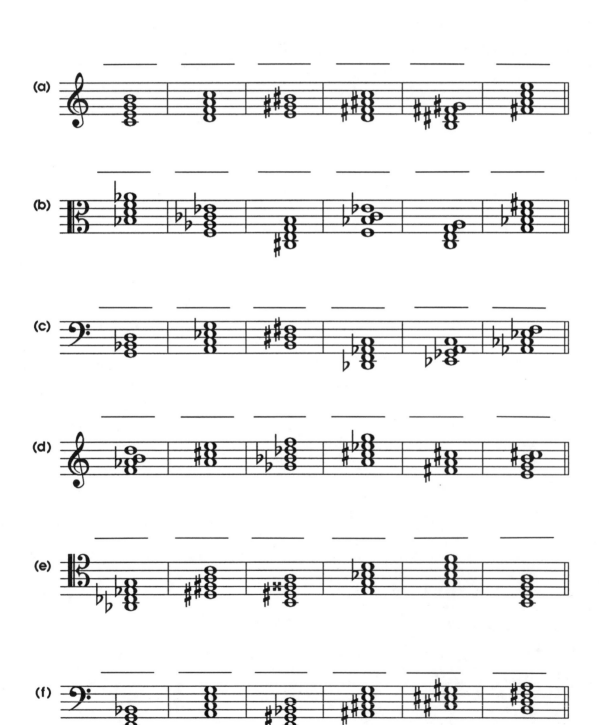

2. *Instructions:* Supply the designated mixed-quality triads and seventh chords on the staffs provided. On diminished triads and fully diminished seventh chords with flatted roots, do not change the root enharmonically; however, do take the options on the rest of the chord members. Generally, take all options regarding fully diminished seventh chords, whenever possible. Again, as in the previous drill study sheets, various chordal symbols are presented; work to enhance your ability to recognize quickly the various chord qualities found within the chordal system.

PERFORMANCE ASSIGNMENT FOR CHAPTER 10

Instructions: The materials in this assignment are meant to stimulate a creative response involving sight singing and ear training. See the list, *Performance Terms and Expression Names* on pages 257–60.

Suggested Mode of Practice

Without having any written instructions on how to write a variation, write a creative version of each song presented in this assignment. Use a single variation technique, such as rhythmically altering the melody, or use a rhythmic and melodic treatment, as in a combined manner. With a metronome, set your own tempos and sing the given version several times in order to become familiar with the rhythmic version presented. When you write your variation, it would be advantageous to retain a semblance of the original melody. Also, in the example that follows, analyze and compare the original with the extended, jazzy, big-band instrumental variation presented. Attempt to do this assignment away from the piano. The point of the assignment is to allow as much freedom as possible and to encourage and stimulate a more realistic effort to enhance sight-singing and ear training. Enjoy your creativity and do as many different versions as time allows; moreover, select other tunes with which you are familiar and do the same thing. Using this creative approach on a regular basis pays huge dividends. Have fun!

"Three Blind Mice"

Instructions: After working on several versions, place your best effort in the blank measures provided below each song. Feel free to make any time-signature changes as you see fit; moreover, provide only your best manuscript skills. Practice your variation so as to be able to perform it, if called upon to do so.

"Happy Birthday"

"Jingle Bells"

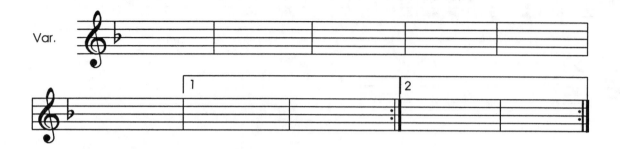

GLOSSARY

The page numbers given indicate where each term is first defined or used. See also *Performance Terms and Expression Marks*, p. 257.

accidentals: the five characters—the natural sign, the sharp sign, the flat sign, the double-sharp sign, and the double-flat sign—used in musical notation to indicate chromatic alterations identify the enharmonic names of the keyboard keys (p. 27)

"add 6" chord: *see* major "add 6" chord, minor "add 6" chord

Aeolian form: one of the three forms of the minor scale; also called *natural form* or *pure form* (p. 116)

Aeolian mode: one of the seven modal scales (p. 64)

alphabetical chord system: a system in which the keynote or root tone of a chord is represented by an alphabetical letter name (p. 218)

altered dominant: the combination of a lowered or raised fifth on a dominant seventh chord (p. 223)

alto clef: a movable C clef used mainly by musical instruments, such as the viola (p. 3)

anacrusis: an unstressed pickup or lead-in note or group of notes that precedes the first accented note of a phrase (p. 202)

augmented interval: a major or perfect interval when made one half step larger (p. 170)

augmented triad: a triad containing a major third and an augmented fifth above its root (p. 220)

bar lines: vertical lines on a staff that specify a measure (p. 35)

bass clef: generally, the lower register of sounds; also called *F clef* (p. 3)

beams: thick horizontal lines joining stems in note-value groupings (p. 69)

beat: the pulse or unit of measure of a composition (p. 34)

binary form: two-part form (p. 229)

blues notes: flatted notes created by lowering various pitches one half step within the scale (p. 197)

borrowed division: the act of borrowing a rhythmic grouping from compound meter and placing it, momentarily, in a simple-time environment, or vice versa (p. 175)

chromatic interval: an interval in which the upper note is altered and is outside the scale scheme of the lower tone (page 170)

chromatic scale: the 12-tone scale, a scale that is created by placing successive pitches one half step apart within one octave and then repeating the starting pitch one octave higher (p. 46)

church scales: *see* modes

clef: a symbol placed on the staff that determines the manner in which the letter names, A, B, C, D, E, F, and G, are assigned to the lines and spaces of the staff (p. 2)

common time (c): $\frac{4}{4}$ time (p. 36)

compound duple: a time signature with two beats per measure, in which the beat is divided into three equal parts (p. 153)

compound interval: an interval that has a range of more than one octave (p. 149)

compound meter: *see* compound time

compound quadruple: a time signature with four beats per measure, in which the beat is divided into three equal parts (p. 153)

compound time: a time signature in which the beat is divided into three equal parts (p. 152)

compound triple: a time signature with three beats per measure, in which the beat is divided into three equal parts (p. 153)

c-one (c¹): *see* middle c

c¹ register: prime register, a range of sounds on the piano keyboard (p. 5)

conjunct: a melodic motion by step (p. 197)

consolidation: the placement of rhythmic elements into beat groupings to eliminate clutter (p. 72)

contra: a range of sounds as shown in Table 1 (p. 5)

c prime (c'): *see* middle c

cut time (¢): $\frac{2}{2}$ time (p. 49)

degree: scale step—either half step (p. 46) or whole step (p. 194)

denominator: the lower number of a time signature that indicates the type of note value that receives the beat (p. 35)

"Diabolus in Musica": the tritone interval of the augmented fourth or diminished fifth (p. 197)

diatonic interval: an interval found in a major scale (p. 150)

diatonic scale: a scale containing a mixture of half steps and whole steps and that is further designated as either a major or a minor scale (p. 90)

diminished interval: a minor interval or a perfect interval (with the exception of the unison) when made one half step smaller (p. 170)

diminished triad: a triad containing a minor third and a diminished fifth above its root (p. 219)

disjunct: a melodic motion by skip (p. 197)

dominant: the fifth degree of each diatonic major and minor scale (p. 118)

Dominant Harmonic Tetrachord No. 5: a tetrachord whose construction is characterized by the one-and-one-half-step interval found between the second and third pitches and which is placed on the fifth degree of the harmonic minor scale (p. 123)

dominant-related triads: triads with alterations that are directly related to the dominant (p. 220)

dominant seventh chord: a chord obtained by adding a minor seventh to a dominant triad (p. 222)

dominant seventh "sus four" chord: a dominant seventh chord in which an interval of a perfect fourth is substituted for the interval of the discarded third (p. 223)

dominant tetrachord: a tetrachord whose starting pitch is located on the fifth degree of a scale (p. 117)

dominant triad: a major triad placed on the fifth degree of the diatonic major or minor scale (p. 222)

Dorian mode: one of the seven modal scales (p. 64)

dot: a rhythmic device for lengthening the duration of a note value or rest value; a dot receives half the value of the note value or rest value that it follows (p. 7)

double flat sign (♭♭): an accidental used to lower a flat pitch by one half step (p. 29) or a natural pitch by one whole step (p. 31)

double sharp sign (×): an accidental used to raise a sharp pitch by one half step (p. 30) or a natural pitch by one whole step (p. 31)

doubly augmented interval: an augmented interval that is made larger by one half step (p. 170)

doubly diminished interval: a diminished interval that is made smaller by one half step (p. 170)

downbeat: an accented beat (p. 49)

duplet: a common two-note grouping in simple time, in which the subdivision, normally in two, is sometimes placed in compound meter (p. 175)

duration: the maximum or minimum length of time that a given pitch is capable of being sustained (p. 2)

ecclesiastical scales: see modes

enharmonic names: alternate names of the keys of the keyboard (p. 27)

enharmonic notes: two or more notes representing the same pitch (p. 31)

equal division: the splitting of four beats into two equal parts within a quadruple environment, a setting in which the upbeat of beat two and the downbeat of beat three are never beamed (p. 70)

F clef: see bass clef

fifth: in a triad or in other chords of larger dimension, the tone that is an interval of a fifth above the root (p. 219)

first ending: the original ending of a section, before the repeat (p. 231)

flag: a curved banner-shaped arc attached to the stem of a note, used to shorten a set duration of time (p. 9)

flat sign (♭): an accidental used to lower a natural pitch by one half step (p. 27) or to raise a double flat by one half step (p. 29)

fully diminished seventh chord: a diminished seventh chord that contains a diminished triad and an interval of a diminished seventh (p. 224)

G clef: see treble clef

Great register: a range of sounds as shown in Table 1 (p. 5)

Great staff: originally, an eleven-line staff, but later divided into two groups of five lines each, representing the bass and treble staffs, joined together by a single line and braced on the left. The two staffs are spaced sufficiently apart to provide for additional pitches and ledger lines. (p. 4)

half-diminished seventh chord: a diminished seventh chord that contains a diminished triad and an interval of a minor seventh (p. 224)

half rest: a rest that is one-half the value of a whole rest (p. 126)

half step: the smallest interval of sound encountered in most music of Western civilization (p. 24)

harmonic form: one of the three forms of the minor scale—obtained by raising the seventh degree of the Aeolian by one half step (p. 116)

harmonic interval: an interval in which two pitches are sounded simultaneously, as can be pictured in a vertical manner (p. 148)

identical pitches: two or more notes representing the same pitch (p. 5)

implied eleventh line: the center line of the original eleven-line Great staff, now reduced to a ledger line, only to be used when needed by either clef (p. 4)

impressionism: in music, the use of the whole-tone scale to enable lush harmonies, subtle rhythms, and unusual tonal colors to evoke moods and impressions (p. 194)

instant modal transposition: a method for determining which key signature should apply to a transposed mode, based upon the relationship of scale degrees within the Ionian mode (p. 200) *interval:* the distance of sound between two pitches (p. 24)

interval identification: the means by which intervals are measured and classified (p. 148)

inversion (category): a transposition of intervals whereby major and minor intervals, augmented and diminished intervals, and doubly augmented and doubly diminished intervals are interchanged, whereas perfect intervals remain unchanged (p. 172)

inversion (numerical): a transposition of intervals whereby the octave and prime, the seventh and second, the sixth and third, and the fifth and fourth are interchanged (p. 172)

Ionian mode: one of the seven modal scales (p. 64)

keynote: starting pitch (p. 92)

key signature: the sharps or flats appearing at the beginning of a staff, indicating the scale and key of a composition (p. 90)

keytone: *see* keynote

leading tone: the seventh degree of each diatonic major and minor scale (p. 118)

ledger lines: short lines drawn above or below the staff to represent abbreviated staff lines and thereby extend the range of the lines and spaces (p. 3)

Locrian mode: one of the seven modal scales (p. 64)

Lydian mode: one of the seven modal scales (p. 64)

major "add 6" chord: a chord that contains a major triad and an interval of a major sixth as a seventh substitute (p. 225)

major interval: an interval that is formed by combining the keynote of the diatonic major scale with its second (ninth), third (tenth), sixth (thirteenth), and seventh degrees (p. 151)

major seventh chord: a chord that contains a major triad and a major seventh interval (p. 225)

Major Tetrachord: Tetrachord No. 1 (p. 90)

major triad: a triad in which the distance between its root and its third is major and the distance between its root and its fifth is perfect (p. 219)

measure: a musical expression that is set between two bar lines and that conveys a rhythmic, melodic, and/or harmonic idea (p. 35)

mediant: the third degree of each diatonic major and minor scale (p. 118)

melodic form: one of the three forms of the minor scale—characterized by the raising of the sixth and seventh degrees ascending of the Aeolian form of the minor and the restoring of the original form of the Aeolian by lowering the seventh and sixth degrees descending (p. 117)

melodic interval: an interval in which two pitches are sounded successively, as can be pictured in a horizontal manner (p. 148)

meter: a system of time in which bar lines concisely measure and organize rhythmic invention (p. 34)

metronome: a device that indicates the speed of a musical composition to the composer, conductor, or performer (p. 48)

middle c: a note placed on the implied eleventh line of either the bass or treble staff, also called *c prime* or *c one* (p. 4)

minor "add 6" chord: a chord that contains a minor triad and an interval of a major sixth as a seventh substitute (p. 226)

minor/major seventh chord: a chord that contains a minor triad and an interval of a major seventh (p. 226)

minor seventh chord: a chord that combines the minor triad and the interval of the minor seventh (p. 223)

minor seventh chord with a flatted fifth: *see* half-diminished seventh chord

minor triad: a triad in which the distance between its root and its third is minor and the distance between its root and its fifth is perfect (p. 219)

Mixolydian mode: one of the seven modal scales (p. 64)

modal pitches of the scale: the second, third, sixth, and seventh degrees of each diatonic major and minor scale (p. 118)

modal scales: *see* modes

modes: scales used, originally, in early church music; also called *modal scales, church scales,* or *ecclesiastical scales* (p. 64)

movable C clefs: the alto and tenor clefs, used mainly by musical instruments (p. 3)

musica ficta: a composing device in which adjustments in the upper tetrachord of the scale are imposed upon the Aeolian to produce more conclusive sounding scale forms (p. 116)

natural form: *see* Aeolian form

natural sign (♮): an accidental used to raise a flat pitch (p. 28) or lower a sharp pitch by one half step (p. 29)

note: a symbol placed on a staff to indicate the pitch and duration of a sound (p. 3)

note head: the circular part of the note symbol (p. 7)

note value: a symbol that indicates the duration of time of a note (p. 7)

numerator: the upper number of a time signature that indicates the number of beats within a measure (p. 34)

octave: a distance of eight letter names—for example: c, d, e, f, g, a, b, c (p. 8); an interval containing twelve half steps (p. 24)

over the split: the imaginary split placed between the upbeat of two and the downbeat of three in a measure of quadruple time (p. 97)

parallel minor scale: a minor scale that shares each of the identical tonal degrees of the major tonality to which it is compared (p. 118)

pentatonic scales: five-tone scales (p. 197)

perfect interval: an interval formed by combining the keynote of the diatonic major scale with its prime, fourth (eleventh), fifth (twelfth), or octave degrees (p. 151)

phrase: a short unit of a musical line, somewhat comparable to a clause or a part of a sentence in prose (p. 202)

Phrygian mode: one of the seven modal scales (p. 64)

pitch: the high or low quality of sound that is determined, in essence, by its frequency or number of vibrations per second (p. 2)

prime: see unison

prime register: c¹ register, a range of sound as shown in Table 1 (p. 5)

principles of applications: eight rules governing the modern use of accidentals (p. 27)

pure form: see Aeolian form

quarter rest: a rest whose value is one-quarter the value of a whole rest (p. 127)

register: range of sound (p. 5)

relative minor scale: a minor scale whose keynote is located on the sixth degree of the related major scale and whose key signature is identical to that of its related major (p. 119)

rest value: a symbol that indicates a duration of silence (p. 7)

rhythm: the pattern of movement in time (p. 34)

root: the fundamental pitch of a triad (or chord of larger dimension) whose alphabetical letter name represents the name of the chord (p. 219)

scales: collectively, an organizational system of pitches (p. 46)

second ending: an alternate ending for a section that is substituted for the first ending during the repeat (p. 231)

sharp sign [♯]: an accidental used to raise a natural pitch by one half step (p. 28) or to lower a double sharp by one half step (p. 31)

simple duple: a simple-time signature with two beats (pulses) to the measure (p. 69)

simple interval: an interval within the range of one octave or less (p. 149)

simple meter: see simple time

simple quadruple: a simple-time signature with four beats (pulses) to the measure (p. 69)

simple time: a time signature in which the beat is divided into two equal parts; also called *simple meter* (p. 69)

simple triple: a simple-time signature with three beats (pulses) to the measure (p. 69)

single-line music: music placed on a staff that is meant for one voice or one instrument (p. 9)

small register: a range of sounds as shown in Table 1 (p. 5)

solfeggio: vocal exercises sung to a system of designated degrees of the scale by syllables (do-re-, etc.), rather than by letters (p. 167)

split: the imaginary line referred to in the concept of equal division; the division of a quadruple measure into two equal parts (p. 70)

staff: a group of five horizontal lines and four spaces on which almost all signs dealing with pitch, duration, and performance can be placed (p. 2)

stem: the vertical line attached to the note head (p. 8)

subcontra: a range of sounds as shown in Table 1 (p. 5)

subdominant: the fourth degree of a diatonic major or minor scale (p. 118)

submediant: the sixth degree of a diatonic major or minor scale (p. 118)

supertonic: the second degree of a diatonic major or minor scale (p. 118)

sus four: *see* dominant seventh "sus four" chord

suspension: the placement of a nonharmonic tone on a rhythmically strong beat in place of the normally expected chord tone (p. 223)

syllabication: the division of words (lyrics) into syllables in vocal music (p. 71)

syncopation: the act of giving prominence to a normally unaccented beat or fraction of a beat by lengthening the duration of its sound (p. 97)

tempo: the measurement of speed of a musical composition (p. 48)

tenor clef: a movable C clef used primarily by musical instruments, such as the violoncello (p. 3)

ternary form: three-part form (p. 229)

tetrachord: a series of four-note segments (p. 66)

third: in a triad, the pitch that is a third (interval) above the root (p. 219)

tie: an arc "connecting" the note heads, used as a rhythmic device for lengthening the duration of a note value or rest value, thus achieving the same result as a dot (p. 7)

time signature: a fraction-like representation of two numbers placed one above the other which indicates the meter and which is given at the beginning or point of change of a composition (p. 34)

tonality: the tonal center, or key, as heard in the melodic and harmonic relationships existing between the scale degrees within a major or minor key scheme (p. 198)

tonal tritone: the combination of the fourth and seventh degrees of a major or minor (harmonic/melodic form) scale (p. 198)

tone: *see* pitch

tonic: the first degree of each diatonic major and minor scale (p. 118)

tonic tetrachord: a tetrachord located on the keynote of both major and minor scales (p. 117)

transposition: the moving of melodic or harmonic patterns to other keys of the keyboard (p. 65)

treble clef: generally, the upper register of musical sounds; the G-clef (p. 2)

triad: a three-tone chord, consisting of a root, a tone a third above it, and a tone a fifth above it (p. 219)

triplet: a common three-note grouping in compound meter, in which the subdivision, normally in three, is sometimes placed in simple time (p. 175)

tritone: an interval consisting of three whole tones (p. 197)

twelve-tone (12-tone) scale: *see* chromatic scale

unison: an interval in which both pitches are identical (p. 149)

upbeat: an unaccented beat, generally preceding the downbeat (p. 49)

whole rest: a rest containing the value of a whole note (p. 125)

whole step: an interval of two half steps (p. 25)

whole-tone scale: the division of an octave into six equal parts (p. 194)

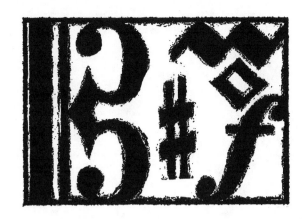

PERFORMANCE TERMS and EXPRESSION MARKS

Term	Abbreviation	Definition
Accelerando	Accel.	with gradually increasing velocity
Adagio	Ad<u>o.</u>	very slow
Ad libitum	Ad lib	at will, at pleasure, or at discretion
A due	a 2	for two instruments
Affetuoso	Afto.	affectionate, with warmth
Agitato	Agt<u>o.</u>	agitated, excited
Al fine		to the end
Alla		in the manner of
Allegro	All<u>o.</u>	quick, lively
Allegro agitato		quick, with agitation
Allegro assai		very fast
Allegro con brio		quick, with brilliancy
Allegro con fuoco		quick, with fire
Allegro con spirito		quick, with spirit
Allegro moderato		moderately quick
Allegro piu mosso		rather quick
Allegro vivace		very quick
Allegretto	All<u>tto.</u>	not as quick as allegro
Andante	And<u>te.</u>	a slow movement
Andante cantabile		slow, but in a singing style
Andante con molto		slow, but with emotion
Andante maestoso		slow, but majestic
Andante ma non troppo		slow, but not too slow

Term	Abbreviation	Definition
Andantino	And^no.	somewhat slower than Andante
Andantino sostenuto		slow and sustained
Animato		with animation and spirit
A piacere		at pleasure, freely performed
Arco		with bow for string instruments
Assai		very, extremely
A tempo	A tem.	in the original time
A tempo guisto		in strict and exact time
Ben marcato		well marked
Bis		to be played twice
Brio		having or showing a joyous mood
Brillante		brilliant, sparkling
Cadence		closing strain
Calando		slower and softer
Cantabile		graceful, pleasing
Circa	ca.	about
Coda	⊕	a second or added ending
Codetta		a coda of small dimension
Comma	,	a place to take a short breath
Con		with
Con forza		with force
Con brio		with vigor and spirit
Con brio ed animato		with brilliancy and animation
Con dolecessa		with delicacy
Con dolore		mournfully
Con energico		with energy
Con espressivo		with expression
Con fuoco		with ardor or fire
Con grazio		with grace and elegance
Con gusto		with exactness and taste
Con moto		with emotion
Con spirito		with spirit, or animation
Crescendo	Cres. ◁	gradually increasing the sound
Da	D.	by, for, from
Da capo	D.C.	from the beginning
Dal segno	D.S.	from the sign
Delicato		delicately
Decrescendo	decresc. ▷	gradually decreasing the sound
Diminuendo	Dim. ▷	gradually diminishing the sound

Term	Abbreviation	Definition
Dolce	Dol.	soft, sweet, delicate
Dolce con gusto		sweetly and with elegance
Double bar	‖	end of a section
Double bar	▌	end of a composition
Elegante		with elegance
Energico		with energy
Espressivo	Express.	with expression
Fermata	⌢	pause (hold)
Fine, fin, or finale		the end of the movement
Forte	f	loud
Fortissimo	ff	very loud
Fuoco		Fire, animation
Furioso		with fire
Glisando		to slide
Grandioso	Grand°.	grand style
Grave		very slow, solemn
Grazioso		smoothly, gracefully
Gruppetto	∾	a group of notes, a turn
Guisto		in strict time, "just right"
Gusto		elegantly
Impetuoso		impetuously
Largo		very slow
Larghissimo		extremely slow
Larghetto		slow, but not as slow as *largo*
Legato		smooth, connected
Lento		in slow time
Lentando		gradually slower and softer
L'istesso tempo		beat remains the same, but meter changes
Maelzel's Metronome	M.M.	instruction for setting a metronome
Maestoso		majestically
Marcato		in strong marked style
Marziale		martial
Meno		less
Meno Mosso		less quickly
Mezzo piano	mp	a little louder than *piano* (half soft)
Moderato	Mod°.	in moderate time
Molto		much or very

Term	Abbreviation		Definition
Morendo			gradually dying away
Mosso			motion
Pausa	⌢		sustaining a rest longer than normal
Piano	*p*		soft
Pianissimo	*pp*		very soft
Piu			more
Piu lento			rather slow
Piu presto			rather accelerated
Poco			a little
Poco a poco			by degrees, gradually
Presto			quick
Prestissimo			very quick
Rallentando	Rall.		slower and softer by degrees
Ritard	Rit.		retardation of time
Segno	𝄋		sign
Sempre			always, throughout
Semplice			simple
Sforzando	*sfz*		with force, with strong accent
Sforzato	*sfp*		a strong accent followed by *piano*
Single bar	|		the beginning or ending of a measure
Smorzanda	Smorz.		dying away by degrees
Sostenuto			sustained
Sotto			subdued, under
Spirito			with spirit, lively
Staccato			short, detached, distinct
Stringendo			accelerating the degree of movement
Subito			quickly
Swing			to play in a jazz fashion
Tacet			silent
Trill	*tr*		rapid alternation of two pitches
Troppo			too much
Tutti			full band or chorus
Tenuto	ten.	(–)	sustained full value
Vivace			quick
Vivo			lively
Volto Subito	V.S.		turn page quickly

SAMPLE SOLUTIONS OF SELECTED DRILL STUDIES

Chapter 1

DRILL STUDY #1, pages 12–13

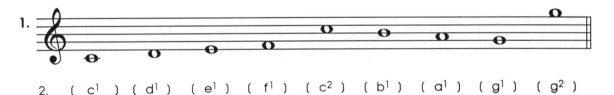

2. (c¹) (d¹) (e¹) (f¹) (c²) (b¹) (a¹) (g¹) (g²)

Only the second bracketed line answers are given. The assumption is that line 1 has already been completed.

DRILL STUDY #2, pages 14–15

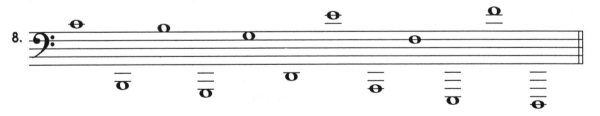

3. (c¹) (BB) (b) (GG) (g) (D) (e¹) (AA) (f) (EE) (f¹) (DD)

Only the third bracketed line answers are given. The assumption is that lines 1 and 2 have already been completed.

Chapter 2

DRILL STUDY #1, pages 39–40

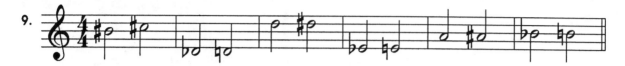

DRILL STUDY #2, pages 41–42

(b♯ / c′ / d♭♭′) (e𝄪 / f♯ / g♭) (a♯ / b♭ / c♭♭′)

Chapter 3

DRILL STUDY #1, pages 55–56

DRILL STUDY #2, pages 57–58

Chapter 4

DRILL STUDY #3, pages 81–82

F Dorian

DRILL STUDY #4, pages 83–84

Chapter 5

DRILL STUDY #1, pages 103–4

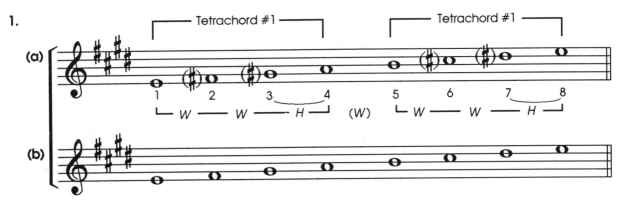

DRILL STUDY #4, pages 109–10

Chapter 6

DRILL STUDY #1, pages 133–34

11. Treble Clef, C Minor, Melodic Form, (Ascending and Descending)

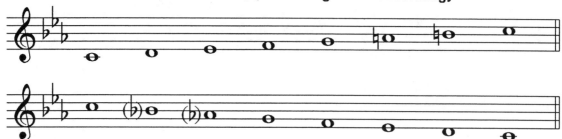

DRILL STUDY #4, pages 139–40

Chapter 7

DRILL STUDY #2, pages 163–64

Chapter 8

DRILL STUDY #1, pages 181–82

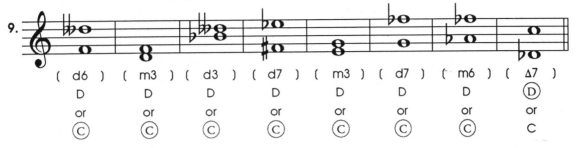

DRILL STUDY #4, pages 187–88

Chapter 9

DRILL STUDY #1, pages 207–8

9. E Whole Tone (Ascending)

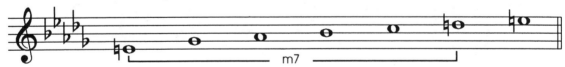

DRILL STUDY #3, pages 211–12

3. F♯ Minor Pentatonic (Ascending)

Chapter 10

DRILL STUDY #2, pages 237–38

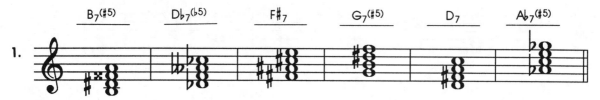

DRILL STUDY #3, pages 239–41

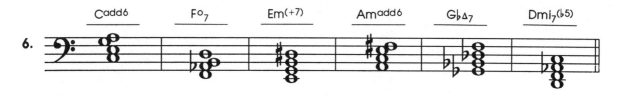

INDEX

Accidentals, 68, 231–32
    placement of, 27–31, 93, 96, 157
    in whole-tone scale, 195–96
"Add 6 chord," 225
Aeolian mode, 64, 66–67, 116–18, 120, 123, 200,
        202, 227
Alphabetical chord system, 218–28
Altered dominant chord, 221, 223
Altered intervals. *See* Intervals
Alto clef, 3. *See* Clef
A major scale, 117
A minor scale, 116, 117, 118
Anacrusis, 202–3
Arc, 177
Ascending form, 117
Augmented intervals, 170–71
    augmented fifth, 220
    augmented fourth, 197, 198
    triad, 220

B, key of, 26, 47, 48
Bar lines. *See* Staff
Baroque music, 223
Bass clef (F clef), 3, 4, 5
Beams, 69–73, 177, 178
Beats, 34–35
    in compound time, 152, 154–55
    division of, 174–78
    groupings of, 72, 155

Black keys, 24
Blues notes, 197
Borrowed division, 175–78
    duplet, 175–76
    tied beamed eighth-note duplet, 127–28
Bracket, 177

C, key of, 26, 47, 48
    C Major scale, 90, 91
    C-one. *See* Middle C
    C-prime. *See* Middle C
Chords, 218–28. *See also* Dominant chords
    Category I. *See* Triad
    Category II. *See* Seventh chords
    Category III. *See* Extension chords
    derivation, 226–27
    symbols, 227
Chromatic intervals, 170–71
Chromatic scale (12-tone), 46–48, 90
Church modes, 64
Circa (ca.), 50
Clef, 2–3, 195
    alto clef, 5–6
    bass clef (F clef), 3, 4
    movable C clefs, 3
    tenor clef, 5
    treble clef (G clef), 2, 4, 5
Common time ($\frac{4}{4}$), 36, 49
Compound intervals. *See* Intervals

Compound meter. *See* Compound time
Compound time, 152–56
    duplet note-value groupings in, 176
    triplet note-value groupings in, 177
    unit of measure, 152
Compound-time signatures, 153–55
    compound-duple, 153
    compound-quadruple, 153
    compound-triple, 153, 154
Conjunct tritone. *See* Tritone
Consolidation of rhythmic elements, 72–73, 98,
    156
Contra registers, 5
Counterpoint, 228
Cut time ($\frac{2}{2}$) *See* Time signatures

Da capo, 229–30
    al fine, 229
    al fine e poi la coda, 230
    al segno, 229–30
Dal segno al fine, 230
Debussy, Claude, 194
Degrees, 5–6, 46, 116, 118, 119, 194
Denominator, 34, 35–36, 97
Descending form, 117, 124
Descriptive language terms, 49–50, 68, 154
    Allegro vivace, 154
    Andante, 50
    Largo, 154
Diagonal notation, 157, 231
Diatonic intervals, 150–51
Diatonic scale system
    major scales, 90, 118, 120–21
    minor scales, 116–20, 118, 120–21
Diminished intervals, 170–71
    diminished fifth, 197, 198, 199, 219, 220
    diminished third, 195
    seventh chords, 221–22
    triad, 219–20
Disjunct tritone. *See* Tritone
D major tetrachord, 92
Dominant chords
    Dominant Harmonic Minor Tetrachord,
        123–24
    dominant seventh chord, 222–23
    dominant tetrachord, 117
    "sus four" chord, 223
    triad, 220–22
Dominant degree, 118
Dorian mode, 64, 65–66, 200–202
Dots, 7, 9, 68, 129

Double flat, 27, 29, 29n, 30
Double sharp, 27, 29n, 30
Doubly diminished interval. *See* Intervals
Downbeat, 49, 70
Duplet. *See* Borrowed division
Duple time, 98
Duration, 2, 7, 97

E, key of, 26, 47, 48
Early music cultures, 197
Ear training, 167
Ecclesiastical modes, 64
Eighth note, 72, 152
Eighth-note rest, 9, 127
Endings, first and second, 231
Enharmonic equivalence, 92, 173–74, 225
Enharmonic names and pitches, 27, 29n, 31–34
Equal division, 69–70, 97–99, 155, 195
    exceptions to, 97–99, 127
    split identification in, 70
Extension chords (Category III), 218, 228

F, key of, 26, 47, 48
F clef. *See* Bass clef
Fermata, 167
Fifth. *See* Intervals
Five-tone scale. *See* Pentatonic scale
Flags. *See* Notes
Flats, 27, 30, 31
    ascending, 46–47, 48, 197
    descending, 46–47, 48
Folk songs, 197
Form. *See* Musical form
Fourth. *See* Intervals

G clef. *See* Treble clef
Great registers, 5
Great staff, 4

Half rests, 126–27
Half step, 24–25, 26, 170
    in chromatic scales, 46–48
    in modal scales, 64
    pattern in modes, 67, 68
Harmonic intervals. *See* Intervals
Harmonic minor scale, 116–17, 120, 123–24
Harmony, 35, 46, 228

Identical pitches, 5–6
Imaginary split. *See* Split
Implied eleventh line, 4

Impressionism, 194
Improvisation, 199, 228
Instant modal transposition. *See* Transposition
Intervals, 24–25. *See also* Augmented intervals;
    Diminished intervals
    chromatic, 173
    classification and identification of, 148–51
    compound, 149, 150
    diatonic, 150–51, 173
    doubly diminished, 170–71
    enharmonic, 173–74
    fifth, 151, 170, 219
    fourth, 151, 170
    half-step, 24–25, 26
    harmonic, 148
    inversion of, 171–72
    major, 151, 170–71
    melodic, 148
    minor, 170–71
    perfect, 170–71
    second, 151, 170
    simple, 149
    sixth, 151, 170
    third, 151, 170, 219, 220
    whole-step, 24, 25–26
Intonation, 51
Inversions, 171–72
Ionian mode, 64, 66–67, 92, 200–202

Jazz, 197, 228

Keyboard, 24–25, 46
    letter names, 26, 34
    scale degrees, 65
Keynote, 92, 151, 195, 199, 218. *See also* Root tone
Key signatures, 90–92
    instant modal transposition of, 200
    major, 92–96
    minor, 124

Leading tone, 118
Ledger lines. *See* Staff
Locrian mode, 64, 66–68, 200, 202
Lydian mode, 64, 66–68, 200, 202

Maelzel, Johann Nepomuk, 48
Maelzel's Metronome (M. M.), 50
Major intervals, 151, 170–71
Major key signatures, 92–96
Major/minor key signatures, 121

Major scales, 90–96
    chord derivation of, 226–27
    diatonic intervals of, 150–51
    pentatonic, 199–200
    tetrachords of, 90–92
    whole and half step pattern of, 90
Major seventh chords. *See* Seventh chords
Major tetrachord, 90–92
Major triads, 219, 221
Manuscript writing. *See* Notation
Measure, 35
Measured silence. *See* Rests
Mediant, 118
Melodic minor scale, 117, 120, 123–24
Melody, 35, 46
Meter, 34, 35, 68, 174. *See also* Tempo; Time
Metronome, 48–50
Metronome markings, 68, 154
Middle C, 4, 5, 6, 67, 90
Minor chords
    minor seventh, 195, 221–22
    minor third, 219
    minor triad, 219, 221
Minor intervals, 170–71
Minor/major seventh chord, 226
Minor scales, 64, 90, 123. *See also* Modes
    Aeolian form (natural minor), 116, 117
    chord derivation, 226–27
    dominant tetrachord, 117
    harmonic form, 116–17, 227
    melodic form, 116–17, 227
    parallel, 118–19
    pentatonic, 199–200
    relative, 119–22
    tonic tetrachord, 117
Minor seventh chords. *See* Minor chords
Mixolydian mode, 64, 66–67, 200–202
Modal scales. *See* Modes
Modes, 64–68, 200–202. *See also* Minor chords;
    Minor scales
    Aeolian, 64, 66–67, 116–18, 119
    Dorian, 64, 65, 66
    Ionian, 64, 66–67, 92
    letter names of, 64
    Locrian, 64, 66–68
    Lydian, 64, 66–68
    Mixolydian, 64, 66–67
    Phrygian, 64
    synthesis, 66–68
    tetrachord derivation of, 66–68
Movable C clefs. *See* Clef

Musica ficta, 116, 117, 120
Musical form
    Binary and ternary, 229–30, 231
    da capo, 229–30
    dal segno, 230
    the short form, 228

Natural form of the minor. *See* Aeolian mode;
    Minor scales
Naturals, 27–28, 29
    ascending and descending, 46
Notation, 92–96, 177, 194–97, 199–200, 225
    bar lines, 99–100
    clef sign, 37
    descriptive language terms, 49–50, 68, 154
    diagonal and vertical, 157, 231–32
    errors of, 128
    metronome marking, 49–50
    number placement, 177–78
    time signature, 37
    vocal and instrumental, 71
Notes, 3
    beams, 69, 70–73
    borrowed, 175–76
    dots and ties, 7, 9
    dotted, 152
    note head, 7–9
    stems and flags, 8, 68, 71, 177
    subdivided, 174–75
Note value, 7, 8, 68
    errors, 127–29
    groupings, 69, 72, 155, 175–76
Numerator, 34, 36, 153

Octave, 8, 24–25, 67, 149, 151, 170, 194

Parallel major and minor scale forms, 118–19,
    123
Partial rests, 156
Pentatonic scale, 197–200
    notation of, 199–200
Perfect intervals, 150–51, 170–71
    perfect fifth, 221
    perfect fourth, 221
Performance
    mode of practice, 167
    of triplets and duplets, 175–76
Phrase, 202
Phrygian mode, 64, 200, 202
Piano
    exercises, 51

    keyboard, 24–25, 46
    nomenclature and pitch spectrum of, 5
Pitch, 1–6
    alteration of, 24–31, 96
    in chord system, 218–27
    in diatonic minor scales, 116–24
    intervals, 148–51, 170–74
    location on staff of, 3–4
    in major scales, 90–96
    in modal scales, 64–66
    organization of, 46–48
    spectrum, 5
    in whole-tone scale, 194–202
Popular songs, 197
Prime interval, 149
Prime registers, 5
Progressions, chordal, 226
Proper grouping, 71
Pure form of the minor. *See* Aeolian mode;
    Minor scales

Quadruple time, 98, 126
Quarter notes, 49
Quarter rest, 9, 127

Registers, 5–6
Relative minor scales, 119–22, 123
Repeats, 98, 229–31
Rests, 9, 68, 125–28, 156
    dotted, 129
Rest value(s), 7, 8, 125–29
    in compound meter, 156
    errors, 127–29
    in harmony, 129
Rhythm, notation of, 7–9
    anacrusis, 202–3
    borrowed division, 174–78
    equal division, 68–73
    meter, 152–57
    rests, 125–29
    syncopation, 97–98
    time signatures, 34–37, 48–51
Root tones. *See also* Keynote
    flatted, 225
    triads, 219

Scale degrees, 65, 151, 195, 200. *See also* Half
    steps
Scales, 2, 26, 34, 64, 92–96. *See also* Major scales;
    Minor scales; Modes; specific types, e.g.,
    Diatonic

ascending and descending, 46–47, 48
chromatic, 46–48
modal. *See* Modes
piano and voice exercises, 51
whole-tone scale, 194–97
Seventh chords, 151, 170, 218, 221–28, 228
dominant seventh, 220, 222–23
fully diminished, 224–25
half-diminished, 224
major seventh, 225–26
minor/major, 226
minor seventh, 223–24
minor seventh intervals, 221–22
notational alignment, 232
Seventh degree of the scale, 116
Sharps, 27, 28, 30, 31
ascending, 46–47, 48, 197
descending, 46–47, 48
Short form, The, 228–31
Signature (key). *See* Key signature
Silence, 7, 9
Simple intervals, 149
Simple meter. *See* Simple time
Simple time, 152, 154
dotting of rests in, 129
duple, triple, and quadruple, 69–70, 71, 72
triplet note-value groupings in, 176
Singing exercises, 51
Single-line music, 9, 129, 177
Sixteenth note, 73
Sixteenth-note rest, 9
Six-tone scale. *See* Whole-tone scale
Sixty-fourth-note rest, 9
Small registers, 5
Solfeggio, 167
Spirituals, 197
Split, 70, 97
absence of, 99
over the split, 97
Staff, 2
bar lines, 35, 99–100
Great staff, 4
ledger lines, 2, 3–4, 5
pitch location on, 3–4
spaces, 2
Stem. *See* Notes
String instruments, 51
Subcontra registers, 5
Subdominant degree, 118
Submediant (sixth) degree, 118, 119
Supertonic degree, 118

"Sus four" chords, 221
Suspensions, 223
Syllabication, 71
Symbols
accidentals, 27
chords, 218–20, 222, 223–24, 227
clef, 2, 3
denominator equivalency, 35
notes, 9
rhythmic, 9
time signatures, 36
Syncopation, 97–98, 127

Tempo. *See also* Meter; Time
metronome settings, 48
subjective language indicators, 48, 49–50
Tenor clef. *See* Clef
Tetrachords, 66–68, 91–92
ascending and descending patterns, 68
B flat major, 91
C Major scale, 91
D major, 92
dominant, 117
Dominant Harmonic Minor Tetrachord, 123–24
E flat major, 91
F major, 91
G major, 91
tonic, 117
Thirteenth pitch, 25, 46
Thirty-second-note rest, 9
Ties, 7, 9, 68, 70, 127–28
Time. *See also* Meter; Simple time; Tempo
compound, 152–56
duration of, 7
Time signatures, 34–37, 49, 69
abbreviated, 49
common time ($\frac{4}{4}$), 36, 49
compound-time, 153–55
cut time ($\frac{2}{2}$), 36, 49, 72, 126
denominator, 34, 35–36
numerator, 34, 36, 153
point of change, 37
quadruple-time, 126
$\frac{3}{8}$ time, 36
Tonality, 119, 151, 195, 197, 198, 227
Tonal tritone. *See* Tritone
Tonic tetrachord, 117–18
Transposition, 65–67, 200–202
Treble clef. *See* Clef
Triads, 218–21, 222, 228

notational alignment, 231–32
Triplet, 175–76, 177. *See* Borrowed division
Tritone, 197–99
Twelve-tone (12-tone) scale. *See* Chromatic scale

Unison, 149, 151, 170
Upbeat, 49, 70

Vertical notation, 157

Viola, 3
Violoncello, 3

White keys, 24, 26
Whole rest, 125–26
Whole step, 24, 25–26
Whole-tone scale, 194–97
Wind instruments, 51